Korean Architecture

Breathing with Nature

KOREA ESSENTIALS No. 12

Korean Architecture

Breathing with Nature

First Published in 2012 by Seoul Selection
6 Samcheong-ro, Jongno-gu, Seoul 03062, Korea
Phone: (82-2) 734-9567
Fax: (82-2) 734-9562
Email: hankinseoul@gmail.com
Website: www.seoulselection.com

ISBN: 978-89-97639-23-6 04080
Printed in the Republic of Korea

Korean Architecture

Breathing with Nature

KOREA FOUNDATION
한국국제교류재단

Seoul Selection

CONTENTS

Delving Deeper

Introduction

Foreign visitors to Korea today are often struck, above all, by the country's architectural landscape. *Republic of Apartment* was the title of one recent work by a French geographer attempting to make sense of the prevalence of the uniform high-rise apartment blocks she found, both in Seoul and in the Korean countryside. A glance lower down, however, and into a few quieter neighborhoods, palaces, Buddhist temples, and pockets of the countryside, reveals a rich heritage of ancient traditional, colonial, modern, and contemporary architecture. Much of Korea's architectural past has been lost or demolished in the recent rush for modernization, but much still remains. This book offers an introduction to Korea's abundant and unique architectural past and present, combining explanations of the principles behind Korean architecture with introductions to some of the country's finest buildings and structures.

Chapter One sets the scene by explaining some of the ideologies and perspectives at the foundation of Korean architectural tradition. Nature, it becomes clear, was a dominant factor in the combination of philosophical and practical considerations that gave shape to the characteristics found in Korea's iconic wood-framed, tiled structures—which varied surprisingly little between building types, be it a palace, temple, school, university, administrative building, or private home.

Chapter Two provides an outline of the history of Korean architecture, from the first architectural traces of dugouts and lean-tos to increasingly sophisticated wooden frames and technologies. Major philosophical and ideological influences, especially from Buddhism and Confucianism, become clear. Korea's late 19th century collision with foreign powers had a cataclysmic influence on its architecture: international styles proliferated throughout the country afterward.

Chapter Three offers a brief introduction to the basic elements of Korean traditional architecture, and the *hanok*, a term used today primarily to refer to houses built based on traditional style wooden frameworks and tiled roofs. The basic construction process, structural anatomy, and materials used are described.

Chapter Four highlights ten of Korea's best-known and most significant traditional buildings, ranging from Buddhist temples and Confucian royal shrines to landscaped literati gardens and "Enlightenment"-era fortresses. It provides a glimpse of the variety of traditional architecture in Korea and some of the principles that shaped it.

Chapter Five focuses on Korea's early modern architecture, which emerged and developed at a historically traumatic time that culminated in 35 years of colonial domination by Japan but is a crucial—and fascinating—period in the country's architectural history. Its scope extends beyond Japan's withdrawal from Korea and into the mid-20th century, when Korean architects such as Kim Swoo-geun and Kim Chung-up began to create a contemporary architectural identity for the country.

"Architecture, of all the arts, is the one which acts the most slowly, but the most surely, on the soul."

– Ernest Dimnet

1

Chapter One

NATURAL PERSPECTIVE REVEALED

A geographical treatise from the Joseon Dynasty (1392–1910), *Taengniji* (Ecological Guide to Korea) outlines the requirements for identifying an ideal site for human habitation. A propitious site, it says, is one with excellent topography, ecology, wholesomeness, and hills and waters. Topography refers to the layout of the surrounding mountains and rivers; ecology to the things that originate from the ground; wholesomeness to the character of the local inhabitants; and hills and waters to the area's scenic beauty. Of these four factors, three are natural phenomena directly related to the earth. This reflects the extent to which Koreans believed nature influenced the desirability of human habitation; indeed, Korea's traditional architecture is meaningless in isolation from nature.

Although the practice of geomancy that Koreans call *pungsu* was introduced to Korea from China, where it originated under the name feng shui, it is actually in Korea, rather than in China or Japan, that its influence has been most evident. Mountains and rivers are the most important elements in *pungsu*. Mountains are needed for harnessing the wind, while rivers constitute sources of water. According to the East Asian perspective, nature is a world of abundant energy, or *gi* (often known in the West by its Chinese pronunciation, qi), that is constantly moving and changing. The wind transports the energy of the sky to the earth, while water carries the energy of the earth. Thus, a terrain with a proper arrangement of mountains and rivers is the most effective means of harnessing the energy of nature. A site with an abundance of natural energy is propitious, as it is believed that this energy will flow into the people living in a house built there.

Changdeokgung Palace is renowned for its design, which defers to the topography of its terrain.

NATURE: THE MOST FUNDAMENTAL INFLUENCE

The first and most important step in traditional Korean architecture, selecting a building site, involves properly interpreting the topography of the land. Ultimately, the most highly sought architectural sites were those known as *baesan imsu*, a term describing a setting with a high mountain at the rear to block the wind and a wide field in front with a river flowing through it. Such an area held promises of abundance.

Once the site was selected, the ground was leveled and prepared for the construction of the building. At this stage, the most important factor was determining the direction the building should

Hahoe Village, with mountains to the north and a river to the south, demonstrates the *baesan imsu* principle.

face. The modern preference for a southern orientation was not an absolute rule. What the building would look out upon was often more important, indicating that psychological perspectives could take precedence over functional considerations. The scene over which a building looked out was called the *andae*. This was most often a mountain, because mountains are the only natural elements considered to be unchanging and everlasting.

The orientation of a village and individual houses can vary according to the *andae* involved. For example, in the Andong hometown of the renowned Neo-Confucian scholar Yi Hwang (Toegye), all the houses face west toward Mt. Dosan, an especially

Hahoe Village: each house faces in a different direction according to its particular *andae*.

auspicious *andae*. In the famous Hahoe Village, however, where many mountain peaks face different directions, various villagers adopted different mountains from the surrounding landscape for their *andae*, and oriented their houses accordingly. As a result, the houses face in every direction—north, south, east, and west, according to their respective *andae*—giving the village a somewhat disorderly appearance. There exits, however, a very strict—albeit not readily apparent—order, whereby the setting of a building and its orientation are determined by various elements in its natural surroundings.

Why did *pungsu* exert such a powerful influence over the selection of building sites and the placement of structures in Korea? The Korean peninsula, which is covered with countless mountains and rivers, boasts a natural environment particularly well-suited to the principles of *pungsu*. It is almost as if the concept of *pungsu* were created as a means of interpreting the topography of Korea.

Preserving the Spirit of Wood and Stone

After deciding on a building site and orientation, the next step involves laying the foundations and erecting the supporting pillars. For the foundation, stones from stream beds were brought to the building site. Stones were not dressed but laid on the ground in their natural state, with their irregular surfaces intact. In order to secure a wooden pillar on top of a foundation stone, the base of the pillar had to be carved to match the irregular surface of the foundation stone. For this process, called *geurengijil*, a specially designed tool was used to draw the curves onto the base of a pillar, which was then carved with an adze. When the carved wooden base was placed on top of the stone, the two pieces would fit together like meshed gears, locking into each other in such a way that the wood and stone became one. Through this difficult and painstaking method, called *deombeong jucho*, the foundation stones and pillars were laid and erected in such a manner that the natural form of the materials was preserved.

At first glance, this may seem a rather primitive method. In fact, it is based on scientific principles. To place a wooden pillar on top of a stone is easier said than done. The base of a wooden pillar rots easily due to rainwater running down the column and gathering at

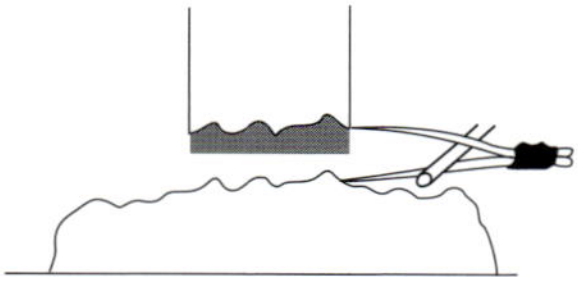

The *geurengijil* technique is used to mark the base of the pillar so that it can be carved to match the contours of its foundation stone.

its footing. To avoid this problem, it is necessary to raise the foundation stone above ground level. In addition, no connecting devices or adhesives can be used between the pillar and the stone because moisture will eventually creep in through the cracks and cause the wood to rot. Accordingly, the only alternative is to position the wooden pillar directly on the foundation stone. In this case, however, any horizontal force, such as earth tremor, a strong wind or a shift in structural load, would cause the pillar to slip off the stone and fall. The only method of construction that can effectively overcome these factors is the *deombeong jucho* method mentioned earlier. Because the irregular surfaces of the stone and wood lock together like meshed gears, the resulting framework is capable of withstanding even horizontal forces.

Wooden columns on foundation stones at Jongmyo Shrine

All the structural pillars placed atop foundation stones are made of wood. Wood is one of the few architectural materials that comes from a living organism; because of its organic nature, it is very difficult and complex to handle. Unlike earth or bricks, wood must be allowed to breathe, can rot from moisture, and is prone to warping. Carpenters who build houses from wood need to understand the nature of this material. For example, wood from trees that have grown on the southern slope of a mountain should be used on the southern face of a house. The same principle applies to trees that have grown on

The complex wooden structure of a palace roof

northern slopes; they should be used for the rear, or shaded side, of the house. This is because wood performs best under conditions similar to its original environment.

Pillars and girders, which bear significant structural loads, should be made from trees that have grown along the timberline. Only trees that have survived the harsh winds high atop a mountain ridge are resilient and sturdy enough to be used for pillars and girders. In contrast, trees that grew in humid valleys with mild temperatures should be used for walls or decorative applications, because their wood is pliable and workable. In order to exploit the ultimate potential of wood, it is necessary to know about the tree's original environment, to such an extent that it was said in the past that expert carpenters did not acquire wood but rather a mountain. The carpenters responsible for building Korea's royal palaces selected a mountain several years before the start of construction and examined the characteristics of the trees from various areas on it before deciding what wood from which tree would be used for each part of the building.

In Korea there is a shortage of thick, straight pine trees. Most pines are thin and crooked. Their bent timber has always been a problem for carpenters. If crooked pines are forcibly straightened out, they become too thin to be used for pillars or any upright elements. The ideal solution was to use the crooked wood in its natural state. On the exterior, this could appear crude and unattractive, but this method brought exceptional structural advantages. Girders and other horizontal elements always have to bear vertical loads from the roof. In extreme cases, when girders cannot withstand downbearing loads, they can collapse. But if wood that is already curved upward is used, there is no danger of it bending downward and breaking under pressure. Furthermore, from a visual perspective, an upward curving wood girder gives an appearance of stability. For this structural reason, wood that curved upward was used for girders and crossbeams in Korean traditional

Daeungjeon Hall, Cheongnyongsa Temple: curved wood has been used in its natural state.

architecture. What began as a functional concept evolved into a notion of aesthetic beauty. Not straight but curved; not fine but coarse—it is this dynamic sense of aesthetics that created the beauty of traditional Korean architecture.

Daeungjeon Hall (Hall of Great Enlightenment) at Cheongnyongsa Temple in Anseong is a textbook example of the number of ways in which curved wood can be used in a building. It contains not a single straight column in any of its four elevations. All columns are crooked and of noticeably different thickness at the top and bottom. Logically, it seems the building should topple over at any minute. However, this structure has been standing firm for over 200 years. The carpenters who built it knew the character of the wood they were using and used it with confidence. In Manseru Pavilion at Seonunsa Temple in Gochang, the crossbeams are all made of beautifully curved wood. Some were even made by joining two pieces of wood together. The interior, with all its twisted girders exposed, has no sense of coziness; rather, it projects an elemental, dynamic feel. Here, we see the application of a different sense of building aesthetics. According to the philosophy of Laozi, who took nature as his model for humanity, "Those things which are finished seem to be unfinished, those things which are straight seem to be bent, and those things which are delicate seem to be clumsy." Such is nature. And so, too, is the appearance of Korea's traditional architecture.

Coping with the Environment

The Korean Peninsula has four very distinct seasons. The coexistence of harsh, cold winters and humid, hot summers creates very difficult natural conditions for coping with architecturally. Indeed, designing a house that can retain heat during the winter as well as keep cool in the summer requires significant expertise and innovation. Korea, furthermore, receives heavy rain and snow, necessitating strong, high-pitched roofs. A strong roof creates a heavy load due to its thick and sturdy crossbeams and columns. Of all the weather conditions in the world, perhaps the most challenging to accommodate in terms of architectural design is the temperate monsoonal climate of the Korean peninsula.

The most exceptional feature of traditional Korean architecture is the integration of *ondol* (heated stone floor) and *maru* (wooden floor). *Ondol* is an underfloor heating system that was developed to provide heat during winter, whereas *maru* is a wooden floor designed to keep interiors cool, especially in humid weather. *Ondol* and *maru*, obviously, have opposing functions. Because an *ondol* floor is heated via underfloor flues, it must be built close to the ground in order to minimize heat loss. A *maru*, on the other hand, must be elevated off the ground in order to reduce humidity. Combining two such very different flooring systems at different

Unheated wooden *maru* (left) and heated *ondol* (right) floors

heights in one particular building is no simple feat. After much trial and error, however, the two were successfully integrated, as can be seen in a *hanok*, the essence of Korean traditional architecture.

Partially heated floor systems, called *kang*, exist in northern regions of China, but only in Korean architecture are heated stone floors and wooden floors combined in the same building, revealing an advanced level of technology and expertise in overcoming extremes of both hot and cold.

Korea receives high rainfall, contributing to its success in rice farming. In the past, however, before the advent of synthetic waterproofing materials, building a leakproof roof constituted a difficult task. For this, a thick layer of earth was laid on the inner roof boards. Although this added weight to the roof, the layer of earth acted as insulation, keeping the house cool in summer and warm in winter.

The most important element in waterproofing, however, is determining the proper slope for the roof. If the slope is too flat, water will accumulate and seep into the building. If it is too steep, tiles may slide off. On a traditional Korean house, the roof curves inward. It was after much experimentation that this concave curve was found to be highly effective in keeping out rain and creating an attractive appearance. This curved roof, which seems to cradle the sky, lifts gently at the edge of its eaves. The resulting curve of the eaves, or *cheoma*, is one of the most elegant aspects of Korea's traditional architecture.

Maksae (end) tiles at the edge of a traditional tiled roof

High levels of skill are required to build such a gracefully curved roof out of

A traditional roof, curving upward at the edges

straight materials. Moreover, the eaves, lifted slightly toward the sky, were not only beautiful but served to moderate interior temperatures. The zenith of the sun is low in winter and high in summer. The slightly uplifted eaves drew sunlight into the house in winter while providing shade in summer, thus helping to keep the interior of the house warm and cool in each of these respective seasons.

The functional aspects of the *ondol*, *maru*, and curved eaves were discovered through experimentation with the laws of nature. Such methods of coping with weather and environmental conditions reveal the wisdom of accepting nature as it is.

Architecture Breathing with Nature

The walls of Korean houses were usually made of earth, using a variety of methods. First, a mold for the front and back was erected, then filled in. By maintaining a wall thickness of about 40 centimeters, the wind could be kept out and moderate temperatures maintained in both winter and summer. Another method involved building a framework of bamboo before applying mud to its front and back. To increase adhesion, bits of straw were sometimes mixed in with the mud; at other times, mud was kneaded with water boiled with kelp and other seaweed. Water boiled with seaweed is an excellent natural waterproofing sealant that is even used in modern construction, as it effectively keeps rain out while allowing stale air and humidity to escape through wall surfaces. When particles of earth are mixed with seaweed water, the spaces between them enable ventilation while keeping out rainwater.

Windows are built into the walls of a house to provide natural lighting, ventilation, and views of the outside. But if the windows are made of wooden slats, these three effects can only be realized when the windows are open. An open window, however, is not a reasonable option in the cold of winter.

How is it possible to maintain a comfortable temperature and

Windows arranged to provide ventilation through optimum use of natural air currents

A traditional interior with the paper-lined windows open (left); close-up of a traditional wooden window pattern lined with *changhoji* (right)

provide natural ventilation and lighting all at the same time? By using *changhoji*, a paper whose name literally means "paper for windows and doors." *Changhoji* is made from the fibers of mulberry bark. It admits and diffuses light. *Changhoji* could be described as a semitransparent material. The sunlight that comes in through it is not direct, but a processed light, so to speak. Thus filtered, the light is milky and comfortable on the eye. It is neither hot nor glaring. The paper prevents the warm air from escaping outside. The use of *changhoji* means that the interiors of traditional Korean buildings are neither bright nor dark.

The fine spaces between the *changhoji* fibers block out strong winds but allow the passing of fine air particles. In a traditional Korean house with a well-designed system of windows and doors, it is said that a person will never catch a cold. *Changhoji* prevents cold air from the outside from coming in, but allows a certain amount of fresh air to circulate through the house. Such natural lighting and ventilation occur when the windows are closed—an effect that can only occur with paper windows. When glass windows are closed, lighting is possible, but not ventilation.

Natural Influences on Architecture

In all the processes involved in building a traditional Korean house—selecting the site, erecting the framework, adding the roof, and installing the doors and windows—the most important consideration was respect for nature. In traditional Korean architecture, nature was not something to be conquered or overcome; it was the model and the ideal standard for everything in the human world. The concept of "untouched nature" in Taosim does not mean going back to primitive times, but rather the creation of a safe and sound world by following the principles of and submitting to the laws of nature. Neither, however, does it mean unconditional adaptation to nature. In Neo-Confucianism, the idea of "human and nature as one" is emphasized; though architecture is a product of humanity, its technologies should respect the laws of nature, and views of the natural surroundings should be brought inside to make the house a part of nature.

Neo-Confucianism also emphasizes the spirit of restraint and modesty in humanity's attitude toward all spaces and natural resources, which in effect means respect for and coexistence with nature. *Pungsu* is a highly developed system of knowledge and values which maintains that the location of a building site and the orientation of buildings should not conflict with nature. The use of crooked pieces of wood involves a construction method that makes optimal use of the natural characteristics of materials. Earthen walls and paper windows maximize the use of natural materials applied in a scientific manner, making them environmentally friendly. While all these materials are taken from nature, they are used with sensitivity and based on advanced technologies for maximum performance. In contemporary times, when the development of science and technology is so often harmful to our environment, it is worth pausing to take note of traditional Korean architecture's respect for nature.

2

Chapter Two

A BRIEF HISTORY

The backbone of Korean architectural history is made largely of wood. While trees can live for more than 1,000 years, felled timber is dead. It easily falls victim to both fire and water. Fire and rebuilding feature in the history of most major Korean buildings, often due to one of the catastrophic wars suffered during the peninsula's long history. Even National Treasure No. 1, Seoul's iconic Sungnyemun Gate, was destroyed by an arsonist in just a few hours on one winter's night in 2008 after standing for five centuries as Seoul's oldest wooden structure. This, combined with a relative lack of written material about architects, buildings, materials, and theory, means that the history of Korean architecture fades relatively quickly into the mist of the past, particularly when it comes to any period earlier than the Joseon Dynasty (1392–1910). A summary of what is known is as follows.

Prehistoric Era

Korean archaeologists have identified several Paleolithic-age (c. 600,000–10,000 BC) dwellings, including early-Paleolithic caves near Pyongyang in today's North Korea. Evidence believed to date from the mid-Paleolithic age suggests that stones may have been used to hold down screen-like shelter walls. Later Paleolithic remains appear to show the use of pillars, fireplaces, and stones from walls and doorways. Many such dwellings are located in sunny spots and close to bodies of water—the latter characteristic thought to be in order to facilitate the hunting of drinking animals. Very little has been discovered of Korea's Mesolithic culture altogether, let alone its architecture, leaving the connection to Korea's Neolithic age (c. 6000–1000 BC) somewhat obscure.

The Neolithic age saw the development of dugout huts, with hardened floors, indoor fireplaces, and holes for pillars. Remains of eleven such dwellings, discovered in southeastern Seoul's Amsa-dong in 1975 and thought to date from around 4000–3000 BC, are

Reconstructions of prehistoric dwellings in Amsa-dong, Seoul

A Bronze Age residential site with stones laid to form a fireplace (left); a Bronze Age dolmen (right)

among the best-known examples of these. The dwellings were generally five–six meters in diameter and roughly round in shape, with central fireplaces. They were dug around 1.5 meters down into the earth and covered, above ground, with thatched roofs supported by wooden frameworks. It appears that wooden frameworks grew more sophisticated during this period, graduating from vertical posts converging conically to a single tip to ridged roofs and, eventually, roofs atop timber frame walls.

Korea's Bronze Age lasted from around 1000–30 BC. Dugout dwellings continued to be built during this period, although the increasingly systematic practice of agriculture brought about more developed villages, as well as structures for defense and grain storage. Half-dugout homes with walls built above ground became more prevalent. One enduring legacy of the Korean Bronze Age is a number of dolmens and menhirs in various parts of the Korean Peninsula. Korean dolmen sites contain some of the highest numbers and concentrations of these megalithic burial structures in the world; they are thought to have been erected over the remains of deceased people of high social status.

Walled City-States and Early Kingdoms

As the bronze age continued and iron implements were eventually introduced, walled cities emerged. War and conquest led to the coagulation of city states into confederations, principally the iron age state of Jin in southern parts of the Korean Peninsula (c. 300–200 BC) and Gojoseon in the north and parts of today's northeastern China (origins undetermined–108 BC). As kingdoms emerged in more centralized federations, capitals with palaces, official buildings and urban layouts, of which little remains, were built. The use of dugout and half-dugout dwellings continued, with early documentary evidence suggesting that harsh winters made deeper dugouts more desirable. It appears that log cabins and structures with raised floors also existed at this time.

Three Kingdoms Period

The Three Kingdoms period (57 BC–668 AD) saw the development of more sophisticated, centralized states. Chinese culture, including Confucianism, Taoism, and later, Buddhism, influenced the culture of the three kingdoms: Goguryeo in the north, Silla in the southeast, and Baekje in the southwest. Periodic relocations of capitals by the three states have left remains of walled fortresses in several locations throughout the Korean Peninsula, but they are better known for their architectural legacy of Buddhist

The Korean Peninsula during the Three Kingdoms period (5th century)

A reconstructed stone pagoda at Mireuksaji Temple Site

structures and royal tombs.

Mireuksaji, an early seventh century Baekje temple site, was home to an enormous nine-story wooden pagoda flanked by two stone pagodas. The central wooden structure and eastern pagoda no longer stand, but part of the western pagoda remains and is considered a valuable example of how Baekje craftsmen transferred woodworking techniques to stone. Nothing but the stone foundations remain of the 68-meter-high wooden pagoda, also a nine-story structure, that stood at Hwangnyongsa Temple in neighboring Silla. Said to have been constructed following the defeat of Baekje by Silla in the 660s by Abiji, the same master craftsman that built the wooden pagoda at Mireuksaji, this would have been one of the biggest and most impressive wooden structures ever to have stood on the Korean Peninsula.

In terms of residential architecture, historical documents suggest that class-based roof differences—thatch for the homes of commoners and tiles for official, religious and royal buildings—had emerged in Goguryeo by at least the fourth century AD. Many Goguryeo dwellings appear to have been characterized by raised storage houses for salt, grain, and other foods. The building of separate structures for different functions within the same dwelling complex apparently began at this time, too. Baekje is thought to have followed a similar progression from dugout homes to thatched and tiled dwellings.

Tombs from the Three Kingdoms period have provided valuable architectural and archaeological insight. Those of Goguryeo fall into two types: square, stepped stone pyramids and large earth mounds. Their ceilings demonstrate ingenious engineering solutions to the problem of having to bear great weight from above. Mostly located in today's North Korea, they were collectively designated a World Heritage Site by UNESCO in 2004. Baekje tombs fall into three broad categories, according to their location in one of the kingdom's three historical capitals: those in the Seoul area were

Cheomseongdae Observatory (left); the interior of a Baekje tomb in Songsan-ri (right)

predominantly shallow stepped pyramids built from small stones; those built later, in Ungjin (today's Gongju), consisted of stone or elaborate brick chambers, the latter possibly influenced by southern China's Liang Dynasty (502–557). The Baejke capital was relocated to Sabi (today's Buyeo) in 538; tombs in this area consisted principally of stone chambers accessed via tunnels. Silla tombs from this period were generally earth-covered and fall into four categories: those with wooden, stone and wood, or stone outer coffins (rather than chambers), and those with stone chambers.

Wooden frame building technology and decoration continued to develop during this period, as did stone and brick construction and arch and barrel vault structures. Cheomseongdae Observatory in the Silla capital, Gyeongju, is held up as a masterpiece of stone architecture and astronomical science of its time.

NORTH–SOUTH STATES PERIOD

After Silla defeated Baekje and Goguryeo, it came to coexist on the Korean Peninsula with the northern state of Balhae from the end of the seventh until the early tenth century. This time is often referred to as the North–South States Period.

Gyeongju, the capital of Unified Silla, produced architectural treasures such as Anapji Pond, Bulguksa Temple and Seokguram Grotto (see p. 69) and Hwangnyongsas Temple. Silla Buddhist temples were generally laid out symmetrically along a north–south axis, with two pagodas built in front of the main hall. It was also during this time that eminent monk Uisang returned from studying in China and built Buseoksa Temple (see p. 85). Silla's flourishing Buddhist culture also produced many stunning stone pagodas. The remains of several Balhae Buddhist temples have been found in today's northeastern China and Russia's Primorsky Krai, particularly in the ancient Balhae capital, Sanggyeong.

Yeonggwangtap, a five-story Balhae brick pagoda in China's Jilin Province, is remarkable for its similarity to Silla brick pagodas.

Residential architecture in Unified Silla was subject to well-defined regulations according to social class. These are said to have extended to the number and size of buildings in any complex, permitted roof tiles, materials, decorations, and even furniture. Very little documentary evidence regarding Balhae homes remains, though some palace ruins suggest strong similarities to Goguryeo architecture.

Unified Silla earth tumuli fell into four types: those consisting only of earth; those with earth on a bed of stone, those with earth on a stone "belt" carved with the 12 animals of the Oriental zodiac; and those with stone figures placed outside the belt with zodiac carvings. Balhae tombs were made either from earth, stone or brick.

Bulguksa Temple's famous Seokgatap and Dabotap pagodas illustrate the Silla practice of placing two pagodas in front of the main temple hall.

Goryeo

During the Goryeo period (918–1392), Buddhism enjoyed the status of state religion. Goryeo occupied the Korean Peninsula almost up to the current North Korean–Chinese border. Goryeo's capital, Songdo (today's Gaeseong, in southern North Korea) was home to the kingdom's main palace, Manwoldae. The palace was built on several terraces of varying height, accommodating rather than leveling the land upon which it stood—a feature often found in Goryeo architecture.

A large number of Buddhist temples were built during the Goryeo period, when the fortunes of the state were widely believed to depend upon the help of Buddha. One of the most valuable surviving examples today is Geungnakjeon (Hall of Supreme Bliss) at Bongjeongsa Temple in southeastern Korea. This relatively simple structure, three *kan* wide and four *kan* deep, has a gable roof and a columnar bracket system to support the considerable weight of the heavy roof and tiles. It is considered Korea's oldest extant wooden building, thought to have been built in the late 12th century.

Wooden pagodas of up to nine stories in height are said to have existed in the Goryeo period, though none survive. Stone pagodas, like those of the Unified Silla period, commonly echoed the forms of those of either Baekje or Silla, while a new form that struck a compromise between these two older forms developed in the mid-Goryeo period. Imitation brick and other less common styles of pagoda were also built.

Geomantic principles (known collectively in Korean as *pungsu jiri*) and the concepts of yin, yang, and the Five Phases (*ohaeng* in Korean; *wu xing* in Chinese) played a prominent role in the planning of Goryeo homes. Class-based design regulations existed but may not have been strictly enforced. Wood frame techniques continued to evolve from those of the Three Kingdoms and the

North–South States Period. One observer writing at the time claimed that one or two out of every ten houses in the capital had tiled roofs; the rest were thatched. *Ondol* underfloor heating systems evolved so that fireplaces came to be located on the outside of heated buildings, rather than inside.

While the basic elements of Goryeo wood-framed architecture—foundations, base stones, wall frameworks, walls, windows, roof frameworks, and roof coverings—all largely constituted continuations from those of preceding periods, the system of bracket sets at the top of columns, designed to support the weight of the roof, grew significantly more sophisticated. Bracket sets directly above column heads grew more complex, while an "intercolumnar" system of adding bracket sets on new horizontal timbers running above and between columns also appeared.

Ruins of the Goryeo-era Manwoldae Palace in Gaeseong (left); Geungnakjeon Hall at Bongjeongsa Temple (right)

Gyeongbokgung Palace is largely symmetrical in layout.

Joseon

When General Yi Seong-gye overthrew the Goryeo Dynasty and eventually declared the new Joseon Dynasty, in 1392, a period of Korean history began that would leave by far the most visible and ubiquitous architectural legacy to be found today. Lasting more than 500 years, this era saw catastrophic foreign invasions and not infrequent fires, but many key wooden buildings were rebuilt—often several times—leaving behind a rich portrait of the past. Buddhism was officially repressed—though by no means eliminated—and Neo-Confucianism promoted as the ideological system, undermining the state, society, and culture.

Following his proclamation of the dynasty, Yi wasted no time in establishing a new capital in today's Seoul. Before the end of the century, Seoul's fortress wall and Gyeongbokgung, the city's main royal palace, had been completed. Mountain fortresses were belatedly added to the north (Bukhansanseong, completed in 1711) and south (Namhansanseong, completed in 1626). Several hundred walled towns were also built during this period, protecting various local official and administrative buildings.

Although Gyeongbokgung Palace was built in relatively symmetrical, geometric form on a north–south axis, Changdeokgung Palace (see p. 72) and other palaces made more concessions to the topography of the sites on which they were built, further emphasizing the Korean tradition of incorporating natural features into architectural design. The designs of palaces and other non-Buddhist buildings were simpler, more restrained, and less flamboyant than those from previous eras, a reflection of Neo-Confucian ideology. Seoul's Jongmyo Shrine (see p. 74) is a well-known example of this.

Seonggyungwan, the national university and highest educational institution in the country, was relocated to Seoul shortly after the establishment of the Joseon Dynasty. Like the several hundred smaller *hyanggyo* (state schools) spread throughout Joseon, it combined the functions of a shrine to Confucius and other illustrious Chinese and Korean scholars (*munmyo*), and of a place of education for students preparing to take the civil service examination. *Hyanggyo* were less successful nationwide than private *seodang* and *seowon*. To the north of its three shrine

Nakseonjae in Changdeokgung Palace (left); Namhansanseong Fortress (right)

buildings, Seonggyungwan included study halls, a library, dormitories, and an examination hall, as well as dining, administration, and storage buildings. Like most Joseon architecture, none of the structures exceeded a single story, though individual buildings varied in height according to function and importance.

Jongmyo Shrine and Sajikdan Altar, located to the east and west of Gyeongbokgung Palace respectively, were among the most important building complexes in the ideological running of the Neo-Confucian state. The former housed the ancestral tablets of deceased Joseon monarchs, while the latter was used to conduct rites in honor of the gods of earth and grain.

Though the Joseon Dynasty adopted the promotion of Confucianism and the repression of Buddhism as a national policy, several Joseon monarchs appear to have held Buddhist faith—a number of temples were built during this time, even in the capital. A significant number of buildings, moreover, were restored or added to existing temples. Built in 1458, Janggyeonggak at Haeinsa Temple (see p. 89) is considered one of the highlights of Joseon architecture for technical as well as aesthetic reasons. Intercolumnar

Haeinsa Temple

bracket systems were now in prevalent use for important buildings, including temples.

The middle part of the Joseon era was marred by the Imjin War, a series of Japanese invasions that began in 1592 and continued for seven years. Widespread destruction, including the razing of many buildings, occurred nationwide, while the simultaneous depletion of natural resources meant that recovery was slow even when the war finished. Many impressive buildings did rise from the ashes, however, including Gakhwangjeon Hall at Hwaeomsa Temple in southwestern Korea. This two-story structure is one of the largest Buddhist halls in the country and was built at the end of the 17th and beginning of the 18th century when sufficient funds became available, many decades after Hwaeomsa's burning during the Imjin War.

Two wooden pagodas from the Joseon Dynasty are extant today: Palsangjeon Hall at Beopjusa Temple in central western Korea and Daeungjeon Hall at Ssangbongsa Temple in the far southwest. The former is said to have been first built in 553, burned down in 1579, and rebuilt in 1626. Its five stories are supported by a combination of tall inner columns, one-story outer columns, and transverse beams. Three-story Daeungjeon at Ssangbongsa is said to have been

Gakhwangjeon Hall, Hwaeomsa Temple

Daeungjeon Hall at Ssangbongsa Temple (left); Palsangjeon Hall at Beopjusa Temple (right)

restored once in 1690 and again in 1984, following a fire. It consists of a rising series of columns placed on the bracket sets of columns on the floors below. Stone pagoda construction is generally considered to have continued in the same style as that of Goryeo, without particular stylistic innovation.

Residential buildings were once again subject to detailed, social class-based regulations in the Joseon period. Commoners' homes showed regional variation in terms of room configuration, but they usually consisted of established elements: an *ondol*-heated *bang*, a raised wooden *maru*, and an earth-floored kitchen area. Upper-class homes consisted of a greater variety of structures composed of the same basic elements, including servants' quarters and divided spaces for male and female occupants. Thatched and tiled roofs, too, largely continued to serve as indications of status.

During the later Joseon period, the Silhak ("Practical Learning") movement gathered momentum, flourishing into a renaissance of sorts under monarchs King Yeongjo (r. 1724–1776) and King Jeongjo (r. 1776–1800). The best-known architectural expression of

Hwaseong Fortress, Suwon

Silhak philosophy and technological innovation is Hwaseong Fortress in Suwon (see p. 76), a short distance to the south of Seoul.

The Joseon Dynasty produced a total of 53 royal tombs in various locations well outside the capital. These were situated according to geomantic principles and built according to guidelines from Chinese Confucian texts. The round, grass-covered mounds were surrounded on three sides by walls; tomb complexes also contained various other statues, stone paths, gates, quarters for guards, and small auxiliary buildings.

Korean Empire

At the close of the 19th century, as Korea's sovereignty came under increasing threat from foreign powers, King Gojong proclaimed the Korean Empire in 1897 and became its first emperor. Attempts at wholesale modernization are reflected in several works of architecture from this period, concentrated in Seoul. The introduction of completely new designs, techniques, and materials shattered the centuries-old domination of wooden frames, *bang* and *maru*, and curved roofs and carved stone, irreversibly ushering in a new era of global influence.

The grounds of Deoksugung Palace function as a microcosmic demonstration of the changes undergone in Korea during this period, through buildings such as Jeonggwanheon Pavilion and

(left to right) Jeonggwanheon Pavilion and Seokjojeon Hall at Deoksugung Palace; Dongnimmun (Independence Gate)

Seokjojeon Hall. Outside the palace, Wongudan Altar, built in 1897, was used by the new emperor to perform the rite of heaven, while Dongnimmun (Independence Gate), completed in the same year, further emphasized the end of Korea's status of inferiority vis-à-vis China. Various other buildings employing new, foreign styles also emerged at this time.

Japanese Colonial Period

The Korean Empire came to an end with the forced annexation of Korea by Japan in 1910. Japan's occupation was to last for years, a time during which a host of administrative and public buildings were erected in Western-influenced styles by Japanese architects. The Neoclassical style Government-General Building, built provocatively in front of the main hall of the Gyeongbokgung Palace and within the palace grounds, was completed in 1926. It was controversially demolished by the South Korean government in the mid-1990s. Some of the other major buildings from the colonial period include the old Bank of Korea (1909, just before Korea's official annexation), Seoul Station (1925), and Seoul City Hall (1926). Incheon, Korea's first open port, displays Chinese, Western, and Japanese architecture from the late 19th century onwards.

(left to right) Old Bank of Korea building; former 58th Bank, Incheon; Dongguksa Temple

Japanese architectural influence from the colonial period can also be found outside Seoul, especially in residential and official buildings in southwestern cities such as Gunsan and Mokpo, where several wealthy Japanese merchants resided. Dongguksa Temple in Gunsan is a highly unusual Korean example of a Japanese-style temple.

Post-Liberation

Following Japan's World War II defeat in 1945, South and North Korea established themselves as separate states in 1948. Shortly afterwards, the Korean War (1950–1953) caused extensive destruction in both Seoul and Pyongyang. North Korea rebuilt its infrastructure after the war through a combination of aid from other socialist states and mass mobilizations such as the Chollima Movement. Many architects trained in the Soviet Union and returned duly influenced. Public architecture was normally Stalinist and absolutist, with Pyongyang serving as a thoroughly designed showpiece full of grandiose buildings. These included the neo-historicist People's Palace of Culture; enormous symbolic monuments, memorials, and sculptures, such as the Party Foundation Monument; and forests of apartment blocks. The

A typical Seoul "forest of apartments"

provinces largely contain a mixture of functional administrative apartment blocks and detached homes, the latter often combining traditional elements such as coal- or wood-fired *ondol* heating systems with modifications such as corrugated iron roofs.

In South Korea, rapid economic development that began in the early 1960s triggered mass migration to the Seoul metropolitan region. Military governments struggled to build functional infrastructure, throwing up "matchbox" apartment blocks and low-rise housing units while members of the public took matters into their own hands and threw up favela-like hillside villages using whatever concrete, bricks, timber, and roofing materials were available. Forced evictions became an ugly but commonplace aspect of city life as whole neighborhoods were razed for redevelopment—a process that continues today. The result is that Seoul's skyline is now densely forested with apartment block complexes, many at least 30 stories high. Though not glamorous or particularly imaginatively designed, it has to be admitted that these dwellings are well-heated, plumbed, supplied with electricity, and popular among many Koreans. Real estate speculation, however, has led to high housing prices. Notable public buildings included neo-traditional efforts such as Cheong Wa Dae (the president's official residence) and the building in the grounds of Gyeongbokgung Palace that now serves as the National Folk Museum of Korea, though a wide range of other styles also developed. In the countryside, the New Community Movement brought the replacement of most thatched roofs with tiled alternatives as part of broad infrastructure modernization. Back in Seoul, the 1988 Olympics saw two of Korea's leading contemporary architects, Kim Swoo-geun (1931–1986) and Kim Chung-up (1922–1988), design the main stadium and Olympic Memorial Gate/World Peace Gate, respectively.

Today, Seoul's most famous contemporary buildings include works by top Korean and international architects alike, reflecting Korea's growing engagement with the rest of the world.

Seoul's old and new City Hall buildings; the new building was designed by architect Yoo Kerl.

3

Chapter Three

ANATOMY OF TRADITIONAL ARCHITECTURE

Though major restoration work still takes place from time to time at temples, royal palaces, and historic buildings today, the residential *hanok* is enjoying a minor revival in popularity, with building sites popping up occasionally in older areas of Seoul and parts of the countryside. Books addressing the technical aspects of building *hanok* have appeared in popular stores, demonstrating that the *hanok* is now a contemporary lifestyle option rather than a relic from a bygone era. South Korea is also home to several *hanok* schools, teaching aspiring carpenter-builders the necessary skills for carrying on Korea's architectural tradition. This chapter offers a look at the characteristic elements of Korea's traditional architecture; the process involved in building a basic residential *hanok*; the principal materials used; and the architects involved.

ELEMENTS OF KOREAN ARCHITECTURE

Roof

The roof could be Korean traditional architecture's most distinctive feature. Though widely identifiable by their rows of dark grey tiles, *hanok* roofs can be divided into several principle categories:

***Paljak* (hip-and-gable) roof:** The most advanced style of *hanok* roof to have been developed, *paljak* roofs can be found on many of Korea's best-known traditional buildings, including Geunjeongjeon Hall in Gyeongbokgung Palace. Many important buildings, including palaces, Confucian academies, and the homes of members of the traditional nobility, use this roof type. In highly stratified Joseon society, the *paljak* roof was reserved for the highest class.

***Matbae* (gambrel) roof:** This simple form of roof was the first to be developed in what is now considered to be Korean traditional *hanok* architecture. Perhaps the most important example of a building with a *matbae* roof is the Goryeo-era Geungnakjeon Hall

Geunjeongjeon Hall, Gyeongbokgung Palace

Paljak roof *Matbae* roof *Ujingak* roof *Moim* roof

at Bongjeongsa Temple in southeastern Korea, believed to be Korea's oldest surviving wooden *hanok* building. This style of roof is often found in *sadang* buildings, used for conducting Confucian ancestral rites.

***Ujingak* (hipped) roof:** Found mostly on private homes, the *ujingak* roof can also be seen on palace gates. A well-known example of this is Gwanghwamun, the recently restored main gate of Gyeongbokgung Palace in central Seoul. Most *choga* (thatched) roofs are also built in *ujingak* form.

***Moim* (gathered) roof:** Another type of hipped roof is the *moim*, or "gathered" roof, where each face narrows as it rises to form a tip. This type of roof somewhat resembles the ridges and faces of an umbrella. It is found on polygonal structures such as Hyangwonjeong Pavilion in Gyeongbokgung Palace.

(left to right) A Confucian shrine; Gwanghwamun Gate; Hyangwonjeong Pavilion

Chogajip and Giwajip

Choga (thatched) roofs were popular among farmers and low-income classes in traditional society. Following the autumn harvest, rice straw was cheap and abundant and therefore used as a material for thatching. Certain climbing plants, such as gourds and pumpkins, could also be grown on top of *choga* roofs. One major disadvantage of rice straw, however, was that it could rot and deteriorate quickly when exposed to the elements. To lay a *choga* roof, first, a layer of earth was spread on wooden roof boards, which was followed by a layer of clay mixed with cut grass. Next, rice straw was spread across the roof and tied down.

Giwa (tiled) roofs were more durable than *choga* roofs and used to signify the importance of the building, as well as the higher status of its occupants. In traditional times, Korea had plenty of clay for making tiles and plenty of firewood for fueling tile kilns; this contributed to the popularity of tiles for roofing. For aesthetic reasons, tiles were produced in a variety of shapes and sometimes imprinted with patterns. To lay a *giwa* roof, a thick layer of earth was first spread over the wooden roof boards that had been laid over the purlins and rafters. Alternate interconnecting vertical rows of "male" and "female" tiles were then laid over the earth.

One striking feature of *hanok* is that the roof appears much bigger than the structure underneath. This is to protect the entire building in various types of weather. In summer, *hanok* roofs provide shade with their wide eaves and protect the walls and windows from the monsoon rain; in winter, they offer shelter from wind and snow and help provide a feeling of warmth.

Choga (left) and *giwa* (right) roofs

Columns

Columns can be regarded as the most important part of Korean architecture, inasmuch as they hold up the roof, walls, doors, and windows. In traditional times, a special ceremony called *ipjusik* (column erecting ceremony) was held on the day the columns were first put up. Great care was taken when preparing columns. During construction, they were always oriented according to the aspect of the tree before it was felled to prevent distortion of the column later on. Columns were erected with the original base of the tree at the bottom; this was based on the belief that standing columns upside-down would bring bad luck to the building. Inspecting the knots in the wood can determine the direction of growth; in the case of most columns, the lower end is also likely to be thicker.

A wooden column at Muryangsujeon Hall, Buseoksa, demonstrates *baeheullim.*

Traditional columns can be found in round, square, hexagonal, and octagonal forms. Round and square columns, however, are the most common.

Different forms of column served as indications, to a degree, of social status. Round columns were found principally in royal palaces and Buddhist temples. During the Joseon era, royalty was the only social class permitted to use round columns.

Various techniques were traditionally used in Korea to make columns appear wider at the base than at the top, or to make them bulge in the center.

BAEHEULLIM, GWISOSEUM AND ANSSOLLIM

Korean builders employed a variety of techniques to compensate for the inadvertent optical illusions that could distort the appearance of buildings.

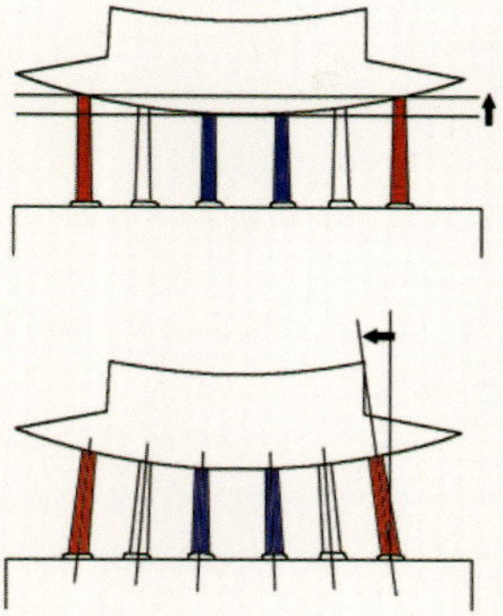
Gwisoseum (top) and *ansollim* (bottom)

Baeheullim is the Korean word for entasis, the practice of making columns wider in their middle sections than at their tops and bottoms. This is generally regarded as an aesthetic device to prevent the column from looking thinner in the center and to give an impression of robust support for the heavy roof. Some have argued, however, that *baeheullim* may have in fact been the aesthetic by-product of making the base of the column narrower in order to reduce the amount of cumbersome preparation work needed for the foundation stone on which it would rest.

Guisoseum literally means "rising at the corners." This term refers to the practice of making the heights of columns in a building progressively taller from the center to the corners, where they are at their tallest. This gradual height increase is of a small magnitude, barely visible to the naked eye, and varies according to the overall scale of the building. It is designed to compensate for the optical illusion that results when the columns are all of uniform height, whereby the outer edges of the building appear to sag.

Anssollim, a term that translates as "leaning inward," describes the way columns are erected at an angle whereby they lean, very slightly, inward toward the building's center. This technique, too, is used to overcome the illusion where absolutely vertical columns at each end of the building appear to lean outward, giving an appearance of instability. This technique was used in the construction of stone pagodas as well as wooden structures.

Ondol and Maru

The principal spaces in a *hanok* all had one of two types of floor: *ondol*, a type of floor heated from below by fire, or *maru*, a type of floor made from wooden boards with empty space beneath. Built above the ground to allow cool air to flow in from below, *maru* floors provided cool spaces in summer. In theory, placing a detached *hanok* in front of a forested mountain would allow relatively cooler air to descend from the mountain in summer and flow across the *maru*, creating a kind of natural air conditioning effect. This type of floor was ideal for the hot, humid parts of the southern Korean Peninsula; it was not originally a prominent feature of houses in the north.

There are several types of *maru* that are named according to the way their floorboards are arranged. A *jangmaru* floor features long, parallel floorboards, while an *umulmaru* is made up of shorter boards, arranged side by side in rows at right angles to longer boards. *Umulmaru* is a type of floor unique to Korea, its structure ideal for preventing the warping that can occur due to Korea's extreme seasonal variations in heat and humidity. It also permits the

Examples of *daecheong* and *toetmaru*

use of shorter planks.

The use of different types of *maru* also varies according to their function and position within a *hanok*. The *daecheong* is normally the largest space in a house, situated in a central position between *ondol* rooms. Such a large *maru* space was needed to conduct *jesa* (Confucian ancestral rites), at which members of the extended family would gather.

The *toetmaru* is a narrower wooden floor that lies between the interior rooms and the ground surrounding the *hanok*. It is built at the same height as the interior rooms and is usually raised to a height above the ground that makes it convenient for a grown adult to sit on its edge. Shoes are removed before stepping onto the *toetmaru*. The *jjokmaru* is a narrower variation of the *toetmaru*, found outside some doors and windows that do not have *toetmaru*. Some upper-class *yangban* homes also featured *numaru*, raised maru floors that functioned like pavilions attached to the rest of the house. Like detached pavilions, *numaru* were normally used to entertain guests and indulge in the appreciation of scenery or composition of poetry.

Less privileged households often used *deulmaru*, which were simple raised wooden platform-like floor surfaces that could be moved around to convenient spots in summer, be it in the shade of a tree or next to a building.

Ondol is often cited as a truly unique feature of Korean architecture. In fact, this fire-based underfloor heating system is a source of cultural pride for Koreans, just as Korea's unique indigenous hangeul alphabet is. It has even been cited by some Korean scholars as proof that parts of today's northeastern China used to be the territory of earlier Korean states due to the archaeological discovery of *ondol* systems there.

An *ondol* floor is made up of large stones, known as *gudeuljang*, covered by clay and a finish usually consisting of impervious oiled

Agungi fireplaces in a kitchen (left); an *ondol* floor

paper. Beneath the floor runs a series of flues that carry hot air and smoke from a fireplace, called an *agungi*, from the adjoining kitchen. The kitchen is located a few feet lower than the room and the chimney on the far side, allowing hot air to rise naturally through the flues, toward the chimney.

The large stones act as storage heaters, so that a hot fire lit in the kitchen for just a few hours can be used to provide a warm floor and, hence, a warm room, throughout a cold winter's night. Koreans often covered the floor with quilts in order to further preserve heat. The occupants of a room would place their legs under the quilt during the day, or their entire bodies at night. *Ondol* is thus thought to have been a contributing factor in the development of the Korean culture of sitting and sleeping directly on the floor, without chairs or beds. Flues beneath the *gudeuljang* were usually arranged either as parallel straight lines or in a fan-like configuration, radiating outwards from the *agungi*. *Gudeuljang* nearer the *agungi* generally had to be thicker than those that were further away, since the heat from the fire was greater.

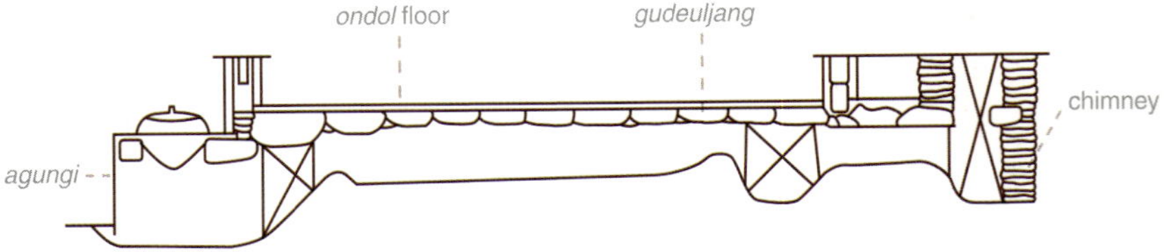

Windows and Doors

The doors and windows of traditional architecture are not always as distinct as those of many Western buildings. Both are usually made of wood and translucent paper and serve to let people in and out of the building, allow air circulation, and admit light. This was accomplished in the absence of glass. Craftspeople specializing in the production of windows and doors are known as *somok*, as opposed to builders of the overall *hanok* structure, who are referred to as *daemok*. These respective terms roughly translate to "small carpenter" and "big carpenter."

Hanok often featured several layers of windows, due to the limited ability of paper to contain heat and cancel noise. These came in a variety of forms, including those that were opened and closed by sliding from side to side (a form still found in most modern Korean windows); those that could be folded, lifted up outwards, and suspended horizontally from the outer ceiling or roof eaves; and other, smaller windows, usually found in auxiliary rooms such as kitchens.

Many *hanok* contain a variety of doors and windows.

Examples of *changsal* and *kkotsal* on windows

The most common type of window body is that made from grids of thin, interlocking lengths of wood, known as *changsal*. This structure combines strength with lightness, allowing the layers of paper stuck to the wooden matrix to admit light without being torn (too easily). *Changsal* also presents opportunities for the creation of intricate and beautiful patterns. Some *hanok* doors and windows even feature *kkotsal*, a highly decorative form that goes beyond the geometric patterns of straight pieces of wood and instead uses ornate patterns of carved flowers. *Kkotsal* is often found in Buddhist temple buildings.

Paper of various thickness is used on Korean doors and windows, sometimes in different parts of the same unit. Thicker paper admits less light and provides better protection from the elements, while thinner paper can be used to brighten the interior.

Hanok doors and windows, though not as structurally important as roofs, columns, or floors, are therefore not only vital in setting the interior atmosphere; they can also make a tremendous impression on the external view of a *hanok* thanks to their abundant capacity for aesthetic expression.

Gates

Gates were another important feature of Korean traditional architecture. Since *hanok* complexes were usually surrounded by walls, gates represented one of the only visible impressions from the outside. Their various forms were used to indicate social status.

Soseuldaemun were initially used only for the homes of public officials, but were later also built also by members of the *yangban* aristocracy, who did not hold office. Their tiled roofs were raised higher than the adjoining tile-topped walls at either side, both indicating the status of their owners and allowing the passing of *choheon*, a sort of sedan chair with a single wheel used by public officials and carried by servants. *Pyeongdaemun*, meanwhile, were used by those that did not hold positions as public officials. Unlike *soseuldaemun*, *pyeongdaemun* did not rise above the level of their adjoining walls.

Important buildings such as palaces, government offices, public schools, and shrines featured triple gates known as *sammun*. In the case of palaces and other buildings used by royalty, the central gate was reserved for the monarch.

A *soseuldaemun* (left) and a *sammun* (right)

Gates are very important in temples, the architecture and layout of which tend to reflect Buddhist principles and beliefs. The entrance and approach to major Buddhist temples feature three main gates. The *iljumun* gate, which has columns and a roof but no door, indicates the beginning of the temple. It has no adjoining walls. Though the *iljumun* is simple in structure and has just two columns, its roof is often ornately decorated. The *sacheonwangmun* houses the Four Heavenly Kings of Buddhism, usually portrayed in the form of large, colorfully painted, and extremely authoritative-looking statues of these four Buddhist gods, each one of whom watches over one cardinal direction of the world. Finally, the *haetalmun* represents the casting off of mental pain and the gaining of enlightenment.

Lastly, the *hongsalmun* is a type of gate that was used to mark the entrance to sacred sites such as royal tombs. It is much lighter in design than other gates, featuring two red columns and a few simple wooden rods arranged vertically as "spikes" along the top span. The *hongsalmun* is said to be red because of a former belief that ghosts disliked this color.

An *iljumun* (left) and a *hongsalmun* (right)

Walls

Very few stone walls remain in Korea's rural villages today. Many were destroyed through lack of appreciation before becoming valued for their aesthetic beauty and the character they lend to human landscapes. Stone walls in villages rarely exceed human height. They were built as symbolic indicators of property limits, rather than absolute physical barriers to keep out intruders. This low height allowed occupants of the houses to look out beyond the bounds of their houses and gardens to the scenery beyond—a highly important part of Korean architecture.

Most traditional Korean walls are built from stone, earth, or brick. Earth walls were the easiest to build, but the least durable. They were usually reinforced by mixing straw and sometimes other elements, such as broken tiles, into the earth. Walls featuring patterned arrangements of broken tiles driven into the earth are known as *wapyeondamjang*, literally meaning "tile fragment walls." Walls featuring highly ornate patterns, sometimes even Chinese characters, were referred to as *kkotdam*, meaning "flower walls."

The famous stone wall of Deoksugung Palace

Examples of patterns in traditional walls

Stone walls, meanwhile, were deliberately built with a degree of irregularity. It was believed that curves rather than straight lines provided greater strength. Gaps between stones, meanwhile, let wind and rainwater flow through, relieving any pressure that would otherwise threaten to knock the wall over.

Hedges were sometimes grown by those without the means to build walls. Thorny plants such as *taengja* (trifoliate orange) and *cheukbaek* (*Thuja orientalis*) were among the popular plant species used. Such hedges were known as *saengultari* or *sanultari*, meaning "living fence." Another popular type of fence was the *ssariul*, made by binding together the slender but tough branches of the *ssari* bush (a type of shrubby bush clover).

Gardens

In traditional times, it was common for even the most ornate *hanok* to be surrounded—up to their outer walls—by almost empty space. These were functional yards, rather than gardens. They were used for household chores, such as threshing rice and drying chiles, and for special social occasions, such as weddings and funerals. Small terraced gardens were sometimes built in the space behind *hanok*, especially in palaces and large mansions.

Koreans traditionally appreciated nature in relatively unaltered

Building a Hanok

1. Determining site and aspect: Korean building tradition holds that choosing a site according to geomantic principles is so important as to constitute "half the building job." Put very simply, the ideal site is on a south-facing slope with a mountain behind and water in front. Needless to say, this is easier to achieve outside of urban areas. Once the site has been chosen, the aspect of the *hanok* must be determined. As already mentioned, most aspects are southerly, perhaps turned to the southeast or southwest to avoid prevailing winds. In some cases, other aspects may be chosen in order to afford views of important mountains in other directions.

2. Groundbreaking and foundation laying: Once the site is chosen, the ground is prepared and the foundation established for the all-important wooden columns. *Hanok* floor plans were principally determined by establishing the distance between columns to create *kan*.

3. Cutting timber: This is perhaps the most important and laborious stage of constructing a *hanok*. Modern power tools have alleviated some of the tedium of bark stripping, planing, meticulous measurement and cutting, and repetitive yet ornate carving, but high levels of skill are still required. Master builder Shin Eung-soo has described the task as "a fight between the wood and the carpenter."

4. Putting up columns and assembly: The base of columns is often carved to mesh exactly with the irregular surface of foundation stones by way of a skilled process known as *deombeong jucho* (see p. 15). When this is done sufficiently well, columns stand straight and stable without additional support. Precut beams, purlins, and other components are then added.

5. Sangnyangsik: The *sangnyangsik* is a ceremony that accompanies the raising of the crucial ridge beam into place. The homeowner, carpenters, and other construction workers conduct a rite for the gods of earth and houses, write the Chinese characters for "dragon" and "turtle," the date, and a short supplication on the beam, and then raise it. A party ensues.

6. Completion and moving in: Following the *sangnyangsik*, the roof, walls, and inner building work are completed and the owner eventually moves in.

forms, however. They often built pavilions in particularly attractive natural surroundings.

There are examples of famous landscaped gardens in Korea, including Soswaewon in Damyang (see p. 79) and Seyeonjeong, the garden of scholar-poet Yun Seon-do (1587–1671), located on the southern island of Bogildo. These gardens are sparser than many of their European counterparts, with fewer trees and plants and a greater emphasis on essential features such as streams, ponds, and existing trees.

Materials

Wood

Pine was considered the best wood for building. Other trees were often collectively referred to as *jammok* (miscellaneous wood). Red pine, regarded as the best of all the pine varieties, was the only wood used in palace construction; Buddhist temples and homes of the elite sometimes also made use of other types of wood, such zelkova, oak, poplar, nut pine, and fir. As with many edible plants in Korea, the use of trees and their timber varied according to their place of origin. Red pines from the deep valleys of Gangwon-do with tall, straight trunks relatively free from knots, were considered the very best for construction. Outstanding trees are still harvested from this area for the reconstruction of major landmarks such as palace buildings and Seoul's Sungnyemun Gate. During the Joseon period, several forests were designated off-limits for civilians in order to protect the supply of timber for royal coffin making, the construction of palaces and other important buildings, naval ships, and other purposes. Paulownia wood, which grows predominantly in the southern regions of the Korean Peninsula, was valued for its resistance to rotting and splitting even when wet.

Geumsan: Forbidden Forests

With the establishment of the Joseon Dynasty in the late 14th century, the royal court introduced a policy ensuring that firewood collection areas and other mountains, forests, streams, and marshes be accessible to the general public. Certain forests, however, were designated *geumsan* (literally "forbidden mountains"; the terms for mountain and forest were used somewhat interchangeably in traditional Korea). These included the mountains around Seoul, the deforestation of which would increase the new capital's susceptibility to natural disasters and interfere with *pungsu* principles. Forests outside the capital were also declared *geumsan* in order to protect valuable timber resources needed by the new state for the construction of palaces and the building of various ships and boats.

Geumsan fell into one of three categories: *gwanbang*, protected in the interests of national defense; *yeonhae*, coastal *geumsan* designated in the interests of construction, shipbuilding, and royal coffin making; and *taebong*, where enclosures were built for storing the placentas of royal family members. Historical records offer only partial information about *geumsan*, but several carved stone notices on mountains designated as such have been discovered, primarily in mountainous eastern Gangwon-do.

Stone

Wooden columns rested upon wider foundation stones known as *juchutdol*. These were usually made of granite and categorized in terms of value and suitability according to provenance. Stone from places such as Pocheon, Gapyeong, Hwangdeung, and Geochang was well-regarded, with Ganghwa *aeseok* (said to be named for the way its color resembled mugwort) among the most popular of all for its color and grain.

Earth and Plaster

Walls were applied in several layers, starting with a mixture of clay, water, and straw (the latter to prevent structural integrity) and followed by one or more outer layers mixed from various clays, sand, and lime or loam. Lime, produced by burning limestone, was an important building material due to its strong adhesive properties.

Tiles

Tiled roofs are often the most visible part of Korean traditional buildings, to the extent that the word *hanok* actually means "Korean roof." After apparently arriving in Korea in around 200–100 BC, roof tiles reached a peak of ornate excellence during Unified Silla. They are made by baking sheets of clay wrapped around round molds at around 800–1,000°C. Kilns were wood-fueled, round, elongated tunnels, half-buried in the ground. On traditional tiled roofs, concave "female" and round "male" tiles are arranged in alternate, interlocking furrows and ridges running down from the roofline to the eaves. Other tiles are used to cap the ends of roof ridges and tile rows.

Thatch

It must be remembered that the majority of Koreans in premodern

Decorated "male" and "female" end tiles on the roof of Gakhwangjeon Hall at Hwaeomsa Temple

times could not afford tiled roofs and instead used rice straw for thatching. Several bundles of straw were spread across the roof, and then held down by a grid-like net of rice straw rope that was tied or weighed down on top of the thatch. Such roofs were vulnerable to damage from wind, rain, and fire—some historical accounts claim that they were replaced on an annual basis, making their long-term costs similar to that of the longer-lasting tile roofs. One advantage of straw thatch was that it was far lighter than tiles, allowing the use of thinner timber in supporting structures. Millet straw, reeds, and other grasses and grain stems were sometimes used.

Continuity

After being marginalized and in many cases actively destroyed during Korea's rapid period of industrialization, traditional building began enjoying a slow return to popularity from the 1990s onwards. Many Koreans hold the view that living in a structure made from natural materials such as wood and *hwangto*, Korea's trademark red clay, brings health benefits. Rediscovered appreciation for traditional culture and aesthetics has also brought some limited benefits to traditional builders, but negative perceptions of traditional houses as cold and inconvenient places to live remain prevalent.

Other obstacles to furthering the building of *hanok* are the lack of suitable timber available in Korea, necessitating imports from countries and regions such as New Zealand, Southeast Asia, and North America, as well as the overall high cost of construction.

Nonetheless, as mentioned above, *hanok* construction has been growing, albeit from a very small base. Wood-based construction showed some dramatic year-on-year increases in the 2000s, although this was not accounted for by *hanok* alone. Increasing demand for such buildings has been accompanied by a need for more builders, leading to a greater number of institutions offering education and training in traditional building techniques.

Perhaps most interesting of all is the question of how the essential elements of *hanok* can be retained and adapted to create well-insulated, modern, reasonably priced, and systematically evolved dwellings that are unmistakably Korean yet indisputably contemporary, thereby unlocking much of Korean traditional architecture from the past.

ARCHITECTS

Joseon-era scholar Song Si-yeol

The professional title "architect" did not exist in Korea until the "modern" era, which is generally considered to have begun between the late 19th century and the end of Japan's forced occupation of Korea (1945). Before this time, as in medieval Europe, the roles of architect and master craftsman were more or less inseparable. The basic design of premodern buildings, whether palaces, temples, schools, or private homes, were remarkably similar in terms of their basic elements, to the extent that the often considerable knowledge of materials, measurements, angles, carpentry, and stonemasonry possessed by craftsmen was sufficient enough for them to build sophisticated, structurally sound structures without additional input from engineers.

Some historians argue that Neo-Confucian scholars in the Joseon era (1392–1910) effectively played the role of architect in designing many of the most outstanding historical buildings that remain with us today. Examples include Dosan Seodang, designed by Toegye Yi Hwang; Dasan Chodang and Suwon Hwaseong, planned by 18th century *Silhak* scholar Dasan Jeong Yak-yong; and Namgan Jeongsa, the work of Uam Song Si-yeol. In the case of many of the buildings in Yi Hwang's hometown, Andong, records indicate that Yi drew plans and supervised construction himself.

In terms of construction, the fact that Korean buildings were predominantly comprised of wooden structures meant that carpenters played the most important role. Carpenter-monks—some with obviously extraordinary levels of skill—are mentioned in historical accounts of the construction of major temple buildings. Still today, it is master carpenters that assume the highest position in projects to reconstruct or restore historical buildings and structures. Carpenters were responsible for identifying, securing, and felling suitable trees, and drying, cutting, and assembling the wood. The literacy rate in premodern Korean society was low, so there are hardly any surviving accounts of their work written directly by craftsmen such as carpenters and stonemasons, who were not part of the literate class. Skills were passed on from master to apprentice verbally or by visual example, as testified by the few carpenter-builders alive today who learned by this method.

4

Chapter Four

KOREA'S MOST IMPORTANT HISTORICAL BUILDINGS

Most of Korea's extant historic buildings date from the Joseon period (1392–1910). A few, such as Bulguksa Temple and Seokguram Grotto, originate from earlier times although such buildings have almost invariably been renovated or rebuilt in the meantime. This chapter introduces ten of the best-known and most valued historical buildings and complexes in Korea. Bulguksa Temple, Seokguram Grotto and Buseoksa Temple are among the best examples of Korean Buddhist architecture in terms of their reflection of religious principles and use of landscape. Jongmyo Shrine is a fascinating embodiment—perhaps the best in the world—of a Confucian royal ancestral shrine, while Changdeokgung Palace and its magnificent garden are considered the most perfect expression of Joseon palace architecture. Yangdong Village gives a glimpse of a very upmarket early Joseon aristocratic neighborhood, while Janggyeonggak at Haeinsa Temple is famous for having preserved invaluable Buddhist woodblocks for centuries. Soswaewon is Korea's most famous scholar garden, while Dosan Seodang and Byeongsan Seowon offer insights into private Confucian academies. Suwon Hwaseong, meanwhile, shows the first traces of Western influence on late Joseon military architecture.

Bulguksa Temple and Seokguram Grotto

The Unified Silla period (668–935) saw a flourishing of Buddhist culture. Silla's capital, Gyeongju, contains many of the nation's most valuable historical and religious treasures. Perhaps best known among these is the Bulguksa Temple and Seokguram Grotto complex, collectively designated World Heritage Sites by UNESCO.

Bulguksa and Seokguram were built between 751 and 790 under the direction and, apparently, according to the plans of former Silla prime minister Kim Dae-seong. Their long building period may have been due to the complex mathematical and geometrical challenges posed by their designs.

Bulguksa Temple

Bulguksa Temple was built as a terrestrial representation of the land of Buddha, or paradise. It achieves this through the creation of three main areas centered respectively on Birojeon (Vairocana Buddha Hall), Daeungjeon (Hall of Great Enlightenment) and Geungnakjeon (Hall of Supreme Bliss). Each hall is raised on a stone terrace. Entry from the mundane world into this heavenly realm was symbolized by the crossing of two stone bridges that punctuate a flight of stone steps leading upwards into the main complex. The main courtyard, in front of Daeungjeon, contains two pagodas: Seokgatap and Dabotap. Dabotap, in the east, is ornately carved and graduates from a square base, through octagonal layers, to top layers that are almost round. Seokgatap, in, the west, is of much simpler design. The two pagodas represent the Dabo and Sakyamuni Buddhas, respectively.

Seokguram Grotto is a granite-lined cave located on the southeastern slope of Mt. Tohamsan, a short distance to the east of Bulguksa. Its interior is dominated by a 3.45-meter-high seated Buddha, looking out to sea. The Buddha occupies a round inner chamber, reached by way of a short corridor, preceded by an antechamber. The antechamber, corridor and walls of the inner rotunda are all carved extensively with Vajradharas, guardian kings, devas, bodhisattvas, disciples, and guardian deities, demonstrating the skill of Silla craftsmen at the time.

Seokgatap and Dabotap pagodas in front of Daeungjeon Hall, Bulguksa Temple

Interior of Seokguram Grotto

Seokguram's architectural significance, however, goes beyond the beauty of its forms and extends to some of its impressive functions and technical aspects. In addition to the remarkable tolerances to which the stone blocks that form the hemispherical dome were carved, the grotto incorporated what appears to have been an effective natural system of dehumidification. The settling of moisture on the Buddha and the surrounding carvings posed the biggest natural threat to their longevity; the grotto was therefore positioned deliberately above a stream on the mountainside. Keeping the floor at a slightly lower temperature than the rest of the structure ensured that airborne moisture condensed on the floor, thereby protecting the rest of Seokguram from dampness and the consequent growth of damaging lichen. Like many other aspects of Seokguram, however, this theory is subject to disputes rendered complicated by preservation efforts in the 20th century that allegedly compromised the original dehumidification system, resulting in a recent damp problem. Another theory is that ten small recesses in the upper part of the walls, which have holes in their bases, allowed natural ventilation, preventing moisture condensation.

Whatever the actual level of scientific knowledge of Seokguram's creators, it and Bulguksa remain outstanding examples of eighth century Silla Buddhist art and architecture and expressions of Buddhist belief at the time.

Changdeokgung Palace

Lying low among the much higher skyscrapers and apartment blocks that dominate the Seoul skyline are the city's five royal palaces: Gyeongbokgung, Changdeokgung, Changgyeonggung, Gyeonghuigung, and Gyeongungung. Gyeongbokgung was the first palace to be built, from 1394–5, and was sometimes referred to as the "north palace." Changdeokgung, known in turn as the "east palace," was completed in 1405 and ended up serving for almost 300 years as the main seat of the dynasty after the destruction of Gyeongbokgung in the Japanese invasion of 1592 (Changdeokgung itself was burned down during the same invasion and again during a political revolt in 1623, but rebuilt both times).

Changdeokgung is remarkable in the way its layout contrasts with that of Gyeongbokgung. While the buildings of the latter are arranged in geometric, parallel fashion, those of Changdeokgung defer to the topography of the terrain upon which they are built, showing a variety of orientations in accordance with the lay of the land. It is also of particular value among Seoul's royal palaces because of its rear garden (*huwon*), a forested recreational area for members of the royal family that is considered one of the best surviving demonstrations of Korean landscape art thanks to its harmonious combination of streams, ponds, forest, and manmade pavilions. It is this combination of architecture, planning, and

Buyongjeong Pavilion, Buyongji Pond, and Juhamnu Pavilion demonstrate the way Changdeokgung Palace's design defers to the topography of its site.

landscape design, as well as its embodiment of geomantic and Confucian principles, that led to Changdeokgung's designation as a UNESCO World Heritage Site in 1997.

Iconic structures in Changdeokgung include Injeongjeon, the main throne hall, and Buyongjeong Pavilion. Injeongjeon was originally built in 1405, but rebuilt twice, in 1610 and 1804, after being burned down. The two-story structure is five *kan* wide and four deep, with multiple intercolumnar brackets on both floors. The stone paved courtyard in front of Injeongjeon contains a central *eodo*, a pathway used only by the monarch, leading directly to the front door of the hall and lined on the left and right by stone markers indicating the positions to be taken by the 24 top-ranking officials in the kingdom. The name "Injeongjeon" means "hall of benevolent politics"—this embodied the newly established Neo-Confucian ruling ideology of the early Joseon Dynasty, where the ideal monarch and government were virtuous, benevolent and well-cultivated.

Buyongjeong Pavilion sits on the edge of—and partly above—Buyongji Pond, further back in a quiet part the palace complex. A cross-shaped structure, it looks out over the pond in such a way that

Aeryeonji Pond and Aeryeonjeong Pavilion, Huwon

the view from inside the pavilion uses architectural features to obscure the ends of the pond, thus giving an impression of infinity. Two of Buyongjeong's supporting columns rest on tall foundation stones that rise out of the pond itself. Though the structure may not appear spectacular, it strikes a balance with the pond, surrounding plants and trees, and nearby buildings.

Jongmyo Shrine

The Yi Dynasty (commonly known as the Joseon Dynasty), which came to the throne in Korea in 1392 and lasted in the form of a kingdom until 1897 (whereupon the monarch declared himself an emperor), was built upon solid Neo-Confucian ideological foundations. Regularly conducted rituals were regarded as crucial for the running of the state; among these, the Jongmyo and Sajik rituals were the most important of all. Having been chosen as the new Joseon capital for its outstanding topographic properties, Seoul was laid out according to strict geomantic principles. Among these was the convention that Jongmyo Shrine be located to the left of the main Gyeongbokgung Palace according to the seated king's point of view (east), and Sajikdan Altar to the right (west). At Jongmyo Shrine, rites were performed in honor of deceased monarchs. At Sajikdan Altar, services conducted were for the benefit of the gods of earth and grain. Both types of rites were regarded as of paramount importance for the fortune of a nation based upon ancestor worship and agriculture.

Jongmyo Jerye rite in progress

Jongmyo's role as a linear series of rooms housing the ancestral tablets of deceased monarchs subjected it to an unusual architectural pressure: it had to be extended as the dynasty survived through time and individual monarchs passed on. Built in 1395, the main hall of the shrine originally contained seven rooms, a number that increased over the years to 19. Like many other shrines, Jongmyo was destroyed during the catastrophic Japanese invasion of 1592—it was rebuilt in 1601. A long, low-lying building displaying only the subdued colors of dark gray roof tiles, dark red columns, and gray-white flagstones in its raised *woldae* ceremonial courtyard, Jongmyo sets a standard for architectural dignity and restraint.

Jongmyo itself was inscribed by UNESCO as a World Heritage Site in 1995, thanks to its having survived in relatively intact form since the early 17th century as an outstanding example of a Confucian royal ancestral shrine. Much of its value, moreover, derives from the fact that Jongmyo Jerye, an elaborate rite featuring rare music, dances, instruments, costumes, and utensils, is still performed there in May every year. The Jongmyo Jerye, too, was inscribed on UNESCO's list of Masterpieces of the Oral and Intangible Cultural Heritage of Humanity in 2001.

Hwaseong Fortress

Located in the city of Suwon, a short distance south of Seoul, is the remarkable Hwaseong Fortress. With stone and brick walls extending for almost six kilometers, the complex is recognized as a remarkable example of 18th century military architecture. Hwaseong's design is attributed largely to Jeong Yak-yong, one of the leading scholars in the silhak movement that gained some influence under the reign of King Jeongjo (r. 1776–1800); the king is said to have been impressed by Jeong's civil engineering prowess and asked him to design and supervise the construction of the fortress. It appears that King Jeongjo intended, by moving the capital to Suwon, not only to secure a military stronghold but to place the seat of royal power in a strategic location with easier access to southern parts of the country, facilitating social, economic, and cultural administration. It was also King Jeongjo's aim to have the move shake off some of the political factionalism of the Seoul court and

Hwaseong Fortress, Suwon

(left to right) Hwahongmun Gate, Seojangdae Pavilion, Dongbuk Gongsimdon

allow the eventual restoration of the reputation of his own father, Crown Prince Sado, who had been tragically executed by King Yeongjo, Sado's father and Jeogjo's grandfather. King Jeongjo had earlier relocated his father's remains to Mt. Hwasan, near the site of Hwaseong Fortress.

Hwaseong Fortress, like Seoul's city wall, has four main gates at the four cardinal points. Unlike the Seoul city wall, however, the northern gate, Janganmun, is considered the main gate because the monarch would enter or exit it on the way from and to Seoul. Each of the gates is further reinforced by a semicircular ravelin structure on the outside. In addition to the four gates, the fortress boasts 44 other defensive features, including floodgates, observation and command posts, towers for firing weapons, secret entrances, beacon towers, bunkers, and more.

As a whole, Hwaseong is celebrated for its groundbreaking combination of military strength, rational structure and functions, aesthetic beauty, and vision of a new type of urban planning. Unlike previous mountain fortresses, which had endured sieges but failed to protect regular towns from being razed by foreign invaders, Hwaseong was designed to protect the whole city. Its walls and gates displayed a variety of innovations of the like never before seen in

Korea, including towers built from brick upon stone foundations with unfamiliar holes and arrowslits. Not content merely with new structures, Jeong created an array of new machines and devices to aid with their construction, including cranes that allowed the raising of heavy rocks and bricks using ropes and pulleys. The construction project, completed in a very brief two years, was also remarkable in that at least half of the total budget was spent on wages for builders and transport workers, a dramatic change from the forced labor that had until then been the norm.

Gates such as Honghwamun, with its seven arches over the northern outflow of the stream flowing through the city, and features such as the beacon tower, with its terraced brick structure, are among the key elements that make Hwaseong so unique and

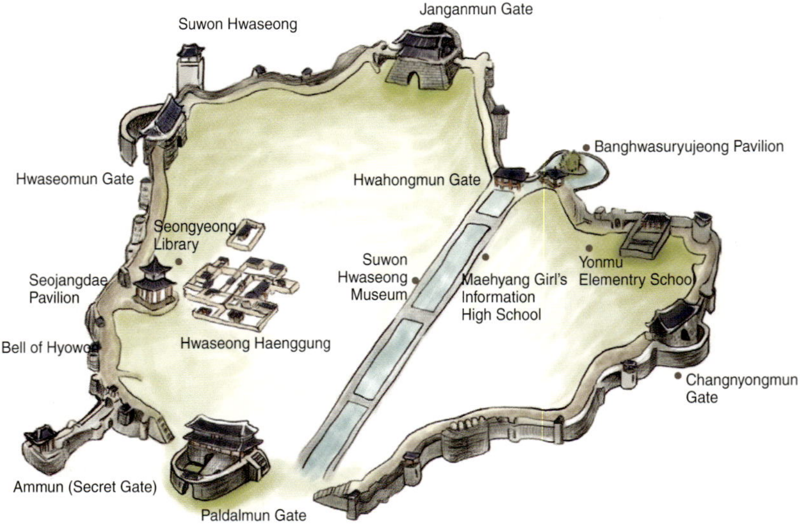

important within the context of Joseon architecture.

Soswaewon Garden

View through Soswaewon to Gwangpunggak Pavilion

That Soswaewon is frequently cited as an outstanding example of Korean traditional architecture is testimony to the intimate relationship between landscape and buildings in Korean culture. Soswaewon is a garden. The small pavilions it contains, though elegant and well constructed, are not generally considered remarkable works of architecture in isolation. It is the interaction between these structures and their carefully designed surroundings that makes the garden as a whole so significant.

The area around Damyang, a small town known for its bamboo crafts, was home of one kind or another to many Neo-Confucian scholars in the early Joseon era (1392–1910). Officials that fell out of favor or whose faction lost the upper hand in the royal court often ended up in exile in the southwestern Honam region; several of the gardens and pavilions they created here remain among Korea's finest examples of Neo-Confucian landscaping and architecture.

Yang San-bo (1503–1557) retired to this area as a young man after failing the civil service examination and seeing his mentor, Jo Gwang-jo, being sent into exile and dying after falling victim to a political purge in the capital. From then on, Yang resolved to remain permanently withdrawn from the world, building himself a private garden to receive guests or spend time in contemplative solitude.

View out from the *maru* of Gwangpunggak Pavilion

Like other such gardens of its time and region, Soswaewon is an expression of ideals and ideology. Its name, meaning a garden of clarity, freshness, and purity (a term applicable both to natural phenomena, such as weather, and human disposition), sets the tone for the subsequent messages and experiences that await visitors.

Soswaewon is typical of a Joseon scholar's private garden in that it is located close to the owner's actual place of residence and contains several pavilions that combine *bang* (room with traditional Korean *ondol* underfloor heating system) and *maru* (open-sided, unheated wooden floor) spaces.

Some researchers have suggested that what remains of Soswaewon today was originally only its "inner garden," and that the "outer garden" continued up the valley in which Soswaewon is located to include elements such as a tea field, peach orchard, bridge, and cave. The inner garden consists principally of three levels, or yards: a middle level, or front yard, at which guests are welcomed upon entrance into the garden; a lower level, or stream yard, designed for socializing, merrymaking, poetry gatherings, and relaxing; and an upper level, or inner yard, designed for quiet study and contemplation with a view out over the whole garden.

Though earlier illustrations indicate a number of buildings now lost, each level of Soswaewon still contains a key pavilion related to its purpose. The front yard is home to a straw-thatched pavilion on a piece of land named Daebongdae: the term *daebong* means "waiting for a pheonix," in which the word pheonix denotes an esteemed guest. A paulownia tree, upon which the pheonix likes to roost, and a stand of bamboo, the fruit of which the pheonix loves to eat, grow here. The stream yard contains Gwangpunggak, a pavilion with *maru* on all four sides of a single-*kan bang*, offering views across the garden, while the higher inner yard is the site of Jewoldang, a smaller pavilion with a smaller *maru*. The *maru* of Jewoldang is raised around a foot higher off the ground than that of Gwangpunggak, a feature that allows a better view down and across the entire garden, thereby emphasizing once again the strong relationship between the buildings in Soswaewon and their surroundings.

Board with calligraphy, Soswaewon

The combined names of Gwangpunggak and Jewoldang (minus the suffixes *-gak*, and *-dang*, which simply indicate the type of building), form a literary quote from the biography of scholar Neo-Confucian philosopher Zhou Dunyi in the *History of Song* (China's Song Dynasty). Zhou's character is described as "like the clear, cool wind that blows and the bracing moonlight in the sky after the rain has stopped," a phrase denoting a clear, bright and virtuous disposition. The garden abounds in further references to literary works and principles central to Neo-Confucian philosophy.

Byeongsan Seowon

Located on a bend in the Nakdonggang River in southeastern Korea, Byeongsan Seowon stands in one of Korea's most traditional areas. Just a few kilometers to the west lies Andong Village, a UNESCO World Heritage Site, while the Andong region as a whole is renowned for its conservatism and well-preserved Confucian heritage.

Although Byeongsan Seowon is one of the top destinations in Korea for those interested in traditional architecture, none of its buildings is particularly noticeable in itself. Best-known is Mandaeru Pavilion, a long, open-sided structure that stands toward the front of the complex looking out over the Nakdonggang River and Mt. Byeongsan beyond, but even this is not the object of any special government designation or preservation order. Some regard Byeongsan Seowon as a demonstration of the fact that Korean architecture is an architecture of gathering, characterized by the collection of buildings and the relationships between them. As has already been mentioned, actual structures themselves varied little,

Aerial view of Byeongsan Seowon from the south

even among buildings with very different uses. When individual structures are regarded as merely parts of the whole, collective building, the open spaces between these structures—such as courtyards, gardens, or ponds—can even be considered interior space, in that they form an inseparable part of the building as a whole. Even the collective "building" is often considered incomplete in isolation from its natural surroundings—a phenomenon that certainly applies in the case of Byeongsan Seowon.

Byeongsan Seowon served multiple functions: as an educational institution, a Confucian memorial shrine, and even a regional center of administration. It was run as the schoolhouse, or *seodang*, of the Ryu family of Andong in nearby Pungsan for several centuries before being relocated to its current site by Ryu Seong-ryong, a top government official, in 1572. The *seodang* was burned down during the Japanese invasion that began in 1592, and rebuilt as a *seowon*—with the added function of a memorial shrine—immediately after Ryu's death in 1607. Byeongsan Seowon was among only 47 such establishments to survive a nationwide mass demolition of *seowon* by 19th century ruler Prince Regent Heungseon Daewongun, with relatively minor restoration works carried out on some of its constituent buildings during the Japanese colonial period (1910–1945). In its heyday as a *seowon* it normally accommodated 20–30 students, all of whom had either passed the first stage of the all-important civil service examination or been otherwise approved by the school's authorities.

While much of Korea's Buddhist architecture can be regarded as centripetal in visual terms, designed with the perspective of outside viewers in mind, many Confucian buildings tend to instead be centrifugal. This is the case with Byeongsan Seowon: from the outside, the long, relatively tall facade of Mandaeru Pavilion dominates the view and offers little perspective regarding the inside. Those looking out to the south from within the *seowon*'s buildings,

Mandaeru Pavilion, Byeongsan Seowon

however, are treated to a descending, layered vista of courtyards, other complex roofs, Mandaeru, and the sandbanks, river, and mountain beyond.

Byeongsan Seowon consists of three principal realms, or clusters of buildings, grouped according to function: the *gangdang*, or educational, cluster to the southwest; the *sadang*, or shrine, complex to the north; and the *juso*, or service/kitchen complex, occupied primarily by servants, to the southeast. The lack of overall symmetry is surprising for a *seowon* complex built at a time when the principles of *yehak*, a system of Neo-Confucian doctrines concerned with etiquette and form, called for symmetry—this is thought to be because the *sadang* cluster was a later addition, not originally factored into the all-important selection of the site. Each of the three clusters in isolation, however, displays almost perfect symmetry among its buildings.

Buseoksa Temple

Considered one of Korea's most outstanding works of architecture for the scenery of which it forms a part, the way its designers made use of the site on which it stands, the interplay between its various buildings, and its Goryeo-era main hall, one of Korea's oldest wooden buildings... Buseoksa is exceptional by any measure.

This Buddhist temple, the name of which means Temple of the Floating Rock, is located in the southeastern province of Gyeongsangbuk-do on the southwestern flank of Mt. Bonghwangsan. Its history is a long one, dating from 676 AD, during the Silla era (57 BC–935 AD). Though many temples later had their construction attributed to the eminent Silla-era scholar-monk Uisang (625–702), records indicate that the only two to which this actually applies are Buseoksa and Naksansa (the latter in northeastern Gangwon-do). After studying in China for five years,

Looking south from Buseoksa Temple

Uisang returned to Korea, where he built Buseoksa and used it as a base from which to spread Hwaeom Buddhism. The floating rock from which the temple gets its name can still be found to the west of the complex; it is said to have been cast down from heaven by Uisang's deceased Chinese ex-lover-turned-dragon to help him overcome local resistance to Buseoksa's construction.

Buseoksa is renowned for possessing two Goryeo-era (918–1392) wooden buildings, of which no more than handful survive in Korea today, as well as for its sublime selection of a site and use of natural features, in conjunction with architectural design, to create such a striking atmosphere. In terms of architectural composition, perhaps its three most noteworthy aspects are the fact that it is built on several stone stages of different levels; that the bent axis along which it is constructed, following one trajectory up to the bell tower and another through the main hall (Muryangsujeon); the elaborate control of perspective shown in the design of Muryangsujeon and other buildings.

Dosan Seodang and Dosan Seowon

Known widely by his pen name, Toegye, Yi Hwang (1501–1570) is perhaps the best-known Korean scholar and philosopher of all time. Also one of the central figures in the country during his own lifetime, he was both a leading Neo-Confucian scholar and a successful politician. His portrait can be found on the front of South Korean 1,000 won notes, while an image of Dosan Seodang was printed on the back of the same note until 2007. Toegye is said to have designed some ten buildings, all for the purpose of study and self-cultivation, in the region of his hometown: today's Dosan-myeon in the jurisdiction of the town of Andong. Dosan Seodang is considered by many to constitute the best expression of Toegye's talent as an architect.

Though Dosan Seodang and Dosan Seowon now form part of the

same complex, the *seodang*, or school, was built first and designed by Toegye himself. Completed in 1560, it consisted of a three-*kan* *seodang* and a larger, eight-*kan* student dormitory, Nongun Jeongsa. Some of Toegye's students later added Yeongnakjae, a second dormitory, further to the southwest. The *seowon* was added behind the *seodang* immediately after Toegye's death, by his students.

Correspondence between Toegye and Beopnyeon, who was in charge of construction of the *seodang*, shows the former rejecting the "工"-shaped plan suggested by the latter. Instead, Toegye demonstrates a firm grasp of practical details not always associated with accomplished philosophers by arguing that such a complicated structure would be hard to roof properly and would compromise the privacy of its occupants by opening lines of sight between its various wings. Toegye opted for almost the simplest conceivable building: a three-*kan*, south-facing structure with kitchen, *bang*, and *maru* in a row, from west to east. On the inside, Toegye pushed the partitioning wall between the *bang* and the kitchen west, reducing

Dosan Seowon and Sisadan

the size of the latter while creating space for a bookcase to hold his large book collection.

Once again, the actual *seodang* structure is only the tip of the architectural iceberg. Though Toegye surrounded most of the yard in front of the *seodang* with a low stone wall, he built a square lotus pond in the southeastern corner with no wall behind it; this opened up the vista from the *seodang* to include the entire landscape beyond, including the Nakdonggang River. To the east, a bridge crossed the small stream that flowed down from the mountain, leading to a garden that Toegye cultivated and used for meditation. Beyond the garden lie various named natural features such as rocks and pools. Anyone dwelling in Dosan Seodang was not cooped up in tiny cramped building, but merely sitting in the middle of an extensive—perhaps even boundless—natural "home."

When Toegye died in 1570, his students were faced with the problem of building a well-situated *seowon* on a site where the original *seodang* already occupied the optimum position. They settled on a site just behind the *seodang*, higher up on the hillside, thereby creating a unified complex that preserved and respected Toegye's *seodang* while according the *seowon* an appropriately higher status. Though Jeongyodang Lecture Hall and Sangdeoksa (the shrine housing Toegye's memorial tablet) are designated National Treasures, the *jeonsacheong* (building used to store food and utensils to be used for rites performed at Sangdeoksa) can be regarded as more architecturally remarkable for the way it divides the building into two halves, each consisting of two *kan*—disregarding the convention of avoiding building structures with even numbers of *kan*. The two halves of the *jeonsacheong* nonetheless contain all the elements ideally associated with such a building; their division allows the line of movement from north to south, between the kitchen quarters and the shrine itself, to flow uninterrupted.

Haeinsa Janggyeonggak

Haeinsa, a large temple on the flank of Mt. Gayasan in southeastern Korea, is reached by following a stunning road that winds up a valley full of large boulders, old trees and a rushing river. In terms of its natural setting, Haeinsa Temple ranks among Korea's most atmospheric temples.

It is better known, however, for another reason: Haeinsa is one of the "Three Jewel Temples of Korea," each of which represents one of the "Three Jewels" of Buddism. Tongdosa represents the Buddha; Haeinsa represents the dharma (Buddhist teachings); and Songgwangsa represents the sangha (Buddhist community). In the case of Haeinsa, the material manifestation of this status is the Tripitaka Koreana, a monumental work of woodblock carvings that record the entire Buddhist canon in Chinese characters, occupying over 80,000 blocks. The carving took place in the 13th century during the Goryeo period; since then, the woodblocks have survived almost without any damage. Their remarkable state of preservation

Main temple courtyard, Haeinsa

Haeinsa Janggyeonggak

is attributed in large part to the buildings that house them. Known collectively as the Janggyeong Panjeon, the four buildings that contain the woodblocks were built in the 15th century and have been designated a UNESCO World Heritage Site in consideration of both their antiquity and their ingenious specialized design.

From the outside, the buildings of the Janggyeong Panjeon are modest in appearance: simple, gable-roofed, and rectangular in terms of floor plan, with none of the colorful decoration that adorns most Buddhist temple buildings and might be expected at the home of one of the greatest treasures of world Buddhism. They are arranged around a long and largely empty rectangular courtyard, with the two longest buildings on the northern and southern sides and the two shorter library buildings at each end. Below their simple tiled roofs, their facades consist only of simple plaster walls with large wooden lattice windows. The simple beauty of their form, however, belies highly effective functions. These structures have proved outstanding at preserving the woodblocks for which they were custom-built. First of all, their location at the top of the temple complex, higher even than the main hall, ensures that their south-facing facades receive adequate sunlight and ventilation. Their floors contain charcoal, calcium oxide, salt, lime and sand, effectively regulating humidity levels all year round. A system of small upper windows and larger lower windows is credited with providing optimal natural ventilation, while the large lower windows in the front facade also serve to admit necessary sunlight but direct it onto the floor, so that the woodblocks receive reflected, rather than direct and potentially damaging, light. The illumination of the floor can also be interpreted as an attempt to transform the necessarily plain earthen floor space that runs along the rows of wooden shelves into a path of light, befitting the religious significance of being in the presence of the dharma jewel.

Yangdong Village

Along with Hahoe Village, Yangdong was collectively inscribed on UNESCO's World Heritage List in 2010, in recognition of their state of preservation and the way they exemplified typical clan villages of the early Joseon era (1392–1910), thereby also serving as embodiments of many aspects of Joseon culture and society.

Yangdong Village is located near the ancient Silla capital of Gyeongju in southeastern Korea. It was established by Son So (1433–1484) of the Wolseong Son clan in 1458. Son's daughter married a son of the Yeoju Lee clan, and Yangdong thereafter evolved around branches of the two clans. The village is built on an extremely auspicious piece of land between mountains, with two waterways flowing in opposite directions and a series of ridges that can be interpreted as resembling the Chinese character 勿, which can in turn be understood to imply everlasting development and prosperity. The village was arranged to reflect its social hierarchy, with the tiled houses of clan families on higher ground and the thatched dwellings of tenant farmers and slaves in valleys and on lower ground.

The Son and Lee clans existed in a somewhat competitive relationship within the village. This is reflected by the presence of two of each major type of building: family manor, pavilion, *seodang* and *seowon*—one for each clan. Perhaps the most striking pair among these, in terms of architecture, are Gwangajeong, built by Son Jung-don (1463–1529), and Hyangdan, built by Lee Eon-jeok (1491–1553). Gwangajeong is defined by restraint and regularity, with a low profile thanks to its site having been dug into the hillside. Seen from below, at the entrance to the village, it appears modest, if somewhat important, but its occupants are treated to dramatic vistas of the surrounding countryside. Its design is simple: a ㅁ shape with two small wings (more like ears) attached to each side of the southern facade, and a separate ancestral shrine is in a walled area in the northeast corner of the compound. With the exception of small *bang* at each corner, most of the ㅁ consists of *maru*, a fact more

Yangdong Village

easily comprehensible when the house is regarded as being primarily used for conducting ancestral rites rather than everyday family life.

Hyangdan, built several decades after Gwangajeong, is different in almost every way: larger, far more ostentatious, and facing a completely different direction. Designed and built by Lee Eon-jeok, it may have been the product of the Lee-Son competition in the village. All of its pillars are round, and many of the wooden elements in its roof are ornately carved, flamboyant features, rarely seen outside royal palaces, that contrast sharply with the restraint of Gwangajeong. A long *haengnangchae* (servants' quarters) constitutes most of the southern, frontal facade. The main house stands immediately behind, on a higher level, so that the view outward from the *maru* of the inner quarters consists largely of the *haengnangchae* roof and the sky beyond. A bird's eye view gives the design of Hyangdan a highly unusual and complicated 巳 shape.

5

Chapter Five

KOREA'S EARLY MODERN ARCHITECTURE

Korea's opening to the West had a profound impact on its architectural landscape. Foreign architectural styles—largely from the West, but also from neighboring countries like China and especially Japan—integrated themselves into the country's skylines. This process accelerated with Japan's forced annexation of Korea in 1910. During their 35-year rule over their neighbor, the Japanese imperialists radically transformed Korea's cityscapes, outwardly "modernizing" urban areas while destroying much of Korea's irreplaceable historical and cultural heritage.

Korea's early modern architecture comes in a wide variety of shapes and forms, reflecting the complex and dramatic nature of its late 19th and early 20th century history. To be sure, much of this architectural heritage is foreign-built, largely by either the Japanese or Western missionaries. A handful of Korean architects were also active during this period—these pioneering artisans formed the first generation of Korean modern architects.

EARLY MODERN ARCHITECTURE?

"Early modern architecture" is, admittedly, a difficult term to define. In the West, "early modernism" is simply part of the larger "modernism" movement. Beginning in the 18th century, this architectural movement reflected the great economic, social, and political upheavals of the 19th century, especially the Industrial Revolution. These dramatic transformations encouraged architects to break with traditional European architectural styles like Gothic and Victorian. Developments in engineering technology also made new forms of architecture possible.

Early modern architectural styles tended to be much more utilitarian than the more ornamental traditional architecture forms. Indeed, over time, architects would come to appreciate the beauty of raw, unadorned architectural materials, Paris's Eiffel Tower being a perfect example. Iron and steel frame construction, the Chicago

Old Seoul Station building

School, Art Nouveau and Art Deco, Soviet constructionism, expressionism, and Bauhaus were widely employed styles of early modern architecture in the West.

In Korea, however, early modern architecture has a very different meaning. Here it is generally defined as architecture—mostly but not exclusively Western-inspired—built between Korea's opening to the West in the late 19th century and the outbreak of the Korean War in 1950, although this is sometimes extended to include modern works built in the 1960s and 1970s. This definition reflects Korea's radically different history of modernization. As was the case in much of the colonized world, modernization in Korea was largely the result of contact with the West, either directly or through a "Westernized" Japan. Unlike the Western modern architectural movement, which reflected social, economic, political, and technological transformations, Korea's early modern architecture reflected the import of foreign concepts and styles. Not all of these

Myeong-dong Cathedral (left) and Seoul Anglican Cathedral (right)

concepts and styles were necessarily "modern," either—two of Seoul's most beautiful pieces of early modern architecture, Myeong-dong Cathedral and Seoul Anglican Cathedral, were built in decidedly traditional Gothic and Romanesque styles, respectively. Korea's early modern architecture also includes works of traditional architecture that have undergone "modern" transformations, such as the *hanok* homes of Seoul's famous Bukchon neighborhood, built in the 1920s and 1930s using modern materials and elements.

Architecture of the Korean Empire

In the late 19th century, Korea found itself under threat by Western imperial powers, China, and increasingly, Japan. France and the United States conducted raids against Korea in 1866 and 1871, respectively. In 1876, Japanese gunboat diplomacy resulted in the Treaty of Ganghwa, in which Korea's Joseon Dynasty opened up its ports to foreign trade. Korea entered into diplomatic and trade treaties with several Western powers soon after.

The opening of Korea had a profound effect on its society. Western (and Japanese) missionaries, diplomats, and traders brought new products, ideas, and institutions. In 1897, Korea's King Gojong proclaimed the start of the Korean Empire, and with it Korea launched a concerted effort to modernize, much as Japan had done following the Meiji Restoration.

Korea's opening transformed the architectural landscape. To be sure, Korea had been importing—and Koreanizing—foreign architecture styles and concepts for centuries, largely from China. In the later part of the Joseon Dynasty, aristocratic Koreans and the royal court introduced exotic elements of Qing Dynasty architecture—such as brick walls and circular windows—into their homes and palaces. The Jipokjae Hall (1888) of Gyeongbokgung

A gate in the grounds of Seokpajeong Pavilion

Palace and Seokpajeong Pavilion (mid-19th century), originally part of the villa of the powerful 19th century Prince Regent Heungseon Daewongun, are among the best examples of this. Korea's opening to the West, however, allowed for altogether new foreign styles to flood in. By 1910, Western-style buildings could be found all over Seoul, including the royal palaces.

Foreign diplomats, foreign businessmen, and Western missionaries were responsible for much of Korean Empire-era architectural heritage, although Korea's imperial court also pushed Western-style construction projects, often hiring Western or Japanese architects to do so. A walk around Seoul's Jeong-dong district, the old Western legation quarter, will reveal a number of graceful buildings from this era, including Victorian Gothic-style Chungdong First Methodist Church (1897); Renaissance-style Jungmyeongjeon Hall (1900), built by a Russian architect as a royal library; the old British Legation (1892), now used as the British ambassador's residence; and the old tower of the Russian Legation

(1890), the rest of which was destroyed in the Korean War. The Daehangno district also has two splendid pieces of Western-style architecture erected at the initiative of the Korean imperial government itself: Daehan Hospital (1907), a beautiful brick edifice with a Baroque clock tower and a Norman entrance designed by a Japanese architect for the Korean Empire's ministry of finance; and the old National Industry Institute (1908), a German-style wooden office also designed by a Japanese architect. Deoksugung Palace itself is home to two beautiful pieces of Korean Empire-era Western architecture: imposing neoclassical Seokjojeon Hall (1910), designed by a British architect as a throne hall for the Korean

(clockwise) Daehan Hospital; Chungdong First Methodist Church; the old tower of the Russian Legation; the old British Legation

Jeonggwanheon Pavilion (left); Pai Chai Hakdang (right)

emperor, and curious Jeonggwanheon Pavilion (1900), built in mixed Korean and Romanesque styles by a Russian architect. Catholic missionaries were also quite active in this period, erecting a number of important churches, including landmark Myeong-dong Cathedral (1898), one of Korea's finest pieces of Gothic architecture.

While foreigners are responsible for much of the Western architecture from this period, Koreans, too, began to learn the new architectural styles. Sim Ui-seok (1854–1924), a Korean traditional architect by training, learned Western architecture through his interactions with Jeong-dong's Western community. He participated in a number of Seoul's major architectural projects from that time, including Western ones (Chung-dong First Methodist Church, Pai Chai Hakdang, Independence Gate, Deoksugung's Seokjojeon Hall) and Korean ones (Wongudan Altar, Gwanghwamun's Bigak and Tapgol Park's Palgakjeong Pavilion).

Architecture of the Japanese Colonial Era

Japan's forceful annexation of Korea in 1910 marked the start of 35 years of foreign imperial rule. The architectural legacy of colonial domination was profound. The colonial authorities undertook massive building projects in order to show off their own power and demonstrate their "modernization" efforts. Korea's cities and towns were transformed, but at great cost to the nation's cultural and historical heritage. This was most painfully demonstrated by the near-complete demolition of Gyeongbokgung Palace, a priceless symbol of Korea's identity as an independent nation, to make way for a massive, neoclassical office to house the Japanese Government-General.

Western architecture had come to Japan only slightly earlier than it did to Korea. Like Korea, the Japanese had initially hired foreign architects to build their early Western buildings and teach the first generation of Japanese architects. For the last two decades of the

Old Bank of Korea building

19th century and first two decades of the 20th, Japanese architects largely employed classical Western styles such as Renaissance and Baroque. Architecture built in Japan's colonies at the time reflects this. The old Bank of Korea building (1912) in Seoul's Myeong-dong district, designed by Tatsuno Kingo, one of the fathers of Japanese modern architecture, is built in French Renaissance style and resembles a French château. Monumental Seoul Station (1925), designed by a student of Tatsuno, is built in Renaissance style, but with a large Byzantine dome. Nakamura Yoshihei's East (1923) and West (1921) Halls of Choong-Ang High School were built in Gothic style. Beautiful Unhyeongung Yanggwan (1912), built as a home for the grandson of Korea's 19th century regent Heungseon Daewongun, employs a Neo-Baroque style.

In the 1920s, however, Japanese architects—inspired by Western architects like Frank Lloyd Wright and Le Corbusier—began to experiment with newer architectural trends like expressionism and rationalism. Japanese architects continued their experiments in the colonies. Seoul Metropolitan Council Building (1935) and the Myeong-dong branch of Shinsegae Department Store (1930) display

Choong-Ang High School (left); Shinsegae Department Store (right)

Old and new Seoul City Hall buildings (left); Incheon Jung-dong Post Office (right)

a modernistic rationalism. The influence of Frank Lloyd Wright can be seen in the horizontal lines and scratch tile of the old Chungcheongnam-do Provincial Hall (1932), while the unusual lines of the old Main Hall of Daegu Medical College (1933) display the influence of German expressionism.

Japanese architects made wide use of eclecticism—the mixture of different historical and national styles to create something completely new. A typical example of this is the old Seoul City Hall (1926), which adds modern elements—for instance, stripped ornamentation—to its classical Renaissance style. A similar mixture of styles is at work in Incheon Jung-dong Post Office.

Korea's first batch of architects trained in Western styles were active in this era, too. One of the best-known is Park Gil-ryong (1898–1943). Graduating from an engineering school in Seoul in 1919, Park cut his teeth with the Government-General's architecture department before forming his own architectural office in 1934. Park's masterpiece, the old Hwasin Department Store (1937), was demolished in 1987, but his flair for modernism and rationalism can be seen in two surviving works, the old Main Hall of Seoul National University (1930) and Kansong Museum of Art (1937). Park also attempted to bring Korean traditional residential architecture, the *hanok*, into the modern era, designing two *hanok* homes—Seoul's Min Byeong-uk House (1938) and Kaksimjae (1938)—with indoor toilets and baths, glass windows, and interior hallways.

Another Korean architect active at this time was Park Dong-jin (1899–1980). Like Park Gil-ryong, he too learned the ropes with the Government-General before forming his own architectural office in 1932. Park is best known for his association with Korean businessman and statesman Kim Seong-su, through whom he came to design the beautiful Tudor Gothic main hall and central library of Korea University (1937). Other works of his, such as the Main Hall of Choong-Ang High School (1937), Youngnak Presbyterian Church (1946), and Namdaemun Presbyterian Church (1955), were similarly built of granite in Tudor Gothic style.

Post-Liberation Architecture

Korea's liberation from Japanese colonial rule in 1945 allowed Korean architects to finally move to the fore. Unfortunately, the early post-liberation era was not an easy place in which to work. Japanese colonial rule had left Korea poor, brutalized, and worse still, divided. The Korean War, waged from 1950 to 1953, left the country devastated. In the reconstruction years that followed, with needs many and resources few, Korea's priorities focused on the practical, not the artistic.

Nevertheless, Korea's first generation of post-Liberation architects still found outlets for its artistic ambitions when the opportunity presented itself. More modern, rational architectural styles, particularly the International Style, also became prevalent beginning from the 1950s. Some architects, however, strove to explore Korean traditional architectural concepts, reinterpreting them in the

Kim Swoo-geun's Freedom Center (left) and Olympic Stadium (right)

language of modern architecture.

Korea's two best known architects from this period were Kim Swoo-geun (1931–1986) and Kim Chung-up (1922–1988). In many ways, the men were a study in contrasts. Educated in Japan, Kim Swoo-geun showed in his earlier work the influence of masters such as Kenzo Tange and Le Corbusier. Later, however, he put much effort into re-understanding Korean traditional architecture, and employing this re-understanding in his work. In his buildings, space and structures flow together, as in Korean *hanok* homes. Kim's close ties with the Korean government afforded him the opportunity to conduct a number of major projects, including the Walkerhill Hotel's Hilltop Bar (1961), the Tower Hotel and Freedom Center (1962) on Mt. Namsan in Seoul, and Olympic Stadium (1984).

Kim Chung-up was a student of Le Corbusier, and much of his work reflects this. His masterpiece, the French Embassy in Seoul (1961), displays the rationalism of Le Corbusier, but the curved roof lines recall the sloped roofs of Korean traditional architecture. Another one of his masterpieces, the Samil Building (1970), is a textbook example of International Style and was Seoul's tallest building for nearly a decade.

Notable Modern Architectural Works

Seokjojeon Hall, Deoksugung Palace

The imposing Seokjojeon Hall of Deoksugung Palace was built to be a symbol of the new, modern Korean Empire. The granite hall, built in the neoclassical style, was built as a throne hall and residence for King Gojong. Construction began in 1900, but the building would not be completed until 1910, long after King Gojong had abdicated. The original design was done by Welsh architect G. R. Harding, but due to the vagrancies of Korea's early 20th century history, a number of architects, including a Russian, a Japanese, another Briton, and Korea's own Sim Ui-seok took part in the project. The portico of Seokjojeon is held up by a colonnade of Ionic columns, while the pediment is ornamented with a relief of a plum blossom, the symbol of the royal family.

Seokjojeon Hall

Jemulpo Club

Jemulpo Club

The city of Incheon was the first Korean port to be opened to foreign trade. Like China's "treaty ports," Incheon—or Jemulpo as it was then known—was divided into several foreign settlements, where foreigners enjoyed extraterritorial rights and ran their affairs virtually independently of the Korean authorities. To this day, Incheon's historic waterfront area is home to many splendid examples of Chinese, Japanese, and Western architecture built during this period.

One of the better examples is the Jemulpo Club, which served as a gathering place for Incheon's foreign community. Completed in 1901, it was designed by Afanasy Ivanovich Seredin-Sabatin, a Russian architect and engineer who authored many buildings in Korea prior to the Russo-Japanese War of 1904–1905. The simple Western-style building sits on a breezy hillside just below Freedom Park (Korea's first Western-style park, also designed by Seredin-Sabatin), with good views over the harbor.

Old Seoul Station

Old Seoul Station

Old Seoul Station served as Seoul's primary gateway between 1925, when the station was completed, and 2004, when a new station was built just next door to handle the recently introduced KTX high-speed train. Along with the mammoth Government-General Building (demolished in 1996), Seoul Station was one of the colonial government's architectural showpieces and for decades one of the city's most prominent sights.

The station building was designed by Tokyo Imperial University professor Tsukamoto Yasushi, a student of Tatsuno Kingo, the pioneering Japanese architect who designed Tokyo Station and Seoul's own Bank of Korea headquarters. Indeed, the Renaissance-style station, with its red brick, granite horizontal accents, and massive dome, is a rather typical example of the "Tatsuno Style" widely employed by the Japanese throughout their empire. Light enters its grand central hall through distinctive Diocletian windows.

After lying unused for several years, the old station was restored and renovated and is now used as a culture and arts space.

Old Seoul City Hall

Along with the Government-General Building and Seoul Station, Seoul City Hall was one of the colonial government's most important showpieces of the 1920s. Completed in 1926, the imposing building is typical of colonial-era eclecticism. Designed in mostly Renaissance style, the reinforced concrete structure also incorporates more modernist elements, most notably its distinct lack of ornamentation. In contrast to the rather austere exterior, the interior is comparatively ornate. Due to the construction of a new City Hall building just behind it, the old City Hall has been renovated for use as a public library.

Chondogyo Central Temple

Completed in 1921, the Chondogyo Central Temple near Seoul's Insa-dong district is the main meeting hall of Korea's indigenous Chondogyo religion. The grand building was designed by the architectural office of Nakamura Yoshihei, one of Japan's leading colonial architects. Its unique Vienna Secession design, however, suggests Nakamura's Austrian-born employee, Anton Feller, had a hand in its authorship. The roof of its cavernous central hall, held up without any pillars, is an impressive piece of civil engineering.

Chondogyo Central Temple (left); Myeong-dong Cathedral (right)

Myeong-dong Cathedral

Located strategically atop a hill in downtown Seoul, massive Myeong-dong Cathedral dominated Seoul's skyline for decades after it first went up in 1898. It was designed by French priest Father Eugene Jean Georges Coste of the Paris Foreign Missions Society, who was also responsible for two of Seoul's other Catholic monuments, Yakhyeon Catholic Church (1892) and Yongsan Seminary (1892). The cathedral, built of red and gray brick by Chinese masons, is a masterpiece of Gothic Revival architecture. With a floor plan laid out in the shape of the Latin Cross, the church has a high vaulted nave flanked by two aisles. In true Gothic fashion, the nave is supported by an arcade, triforium, and clerestory.

The area around the cathedral is rich in early modern architecture, too, including the chapel of the convent of the Sisters of St. Paul of Chartres (1930s), the old church for Japanese worshipers (1928), Coste Hall (1939), the Seoul Archdiocese Annex (1927), and the former archbishop's residence (1890), the oldest extant Western-style building in Korea.

Seoul Anglican Cathedral

Considered one of Korea's most beautiful pieces of architecture and one of the finest pieces of Romanesque architecture in East Asia, Seoul Anglican Cathedral was consecrated in 1926, although the church remained virtually half-finished until its original blueprint was rediscovered in a British library in the 1990s. Church leaders commissioned Arthur Dixon (1856–1929), a British architect and member of the Royal Institute of British Architects, to design the cathedral. The Romanesque monument was designed to blend in with nearby Deoksugung Palace and incorporates a number of traditional Korean elements, especially in its windows and roof. The beautiful gold mosaic behind the altar was done by American-born Scottish designer George Washington Jack (1855–1932).

Old Main Hall of Seoul National University

Completed in 1931, the old Main Hall of Seoul National University is one of the few remaining works of Park Gil-ryong, Korea's first architect trained in Western architecture. The building's modernist style can be seen in its horizontal lines, curved corners and restrained ornamentation. The building is covered in scratch tile, a relief tile invented by American architect Frank Lloyd Wright during his stay in Japan.

Min Ik-du House (now Min's Club)

Also designed by Park Gil-ryong, Min Ik-du House is an attempt to bring Korean *hanok* architecture into the 20th century. The beautiful home near Seoul's Insa-dong district, built in the 1930s, incorporates a number of modern elements into its design, including an indoor entrance, a bath and toilet, glass windows, and interior hallways. It would have been considered breathtakingly modern at the time. The home is now used as a fusion Korean restaurant and café.

Korea University Main Hall and Central Library

The historic Main Hall and Central Library of Korea University were completed in 1937 and designed by Park Dong-jin, one of only a handful of Korean architects active in the Japanese colonial era. The granite buildings, with their distinctive Tudor Gothic design, are said to reflect the wishes of the university's owner and Park's patron, influential Korean businessman Kim Seong-su. In the 1920s, Kim had gone abroad to inspect overseas universities and was reportedly most impressed by North Carolina's Duke University—much of the campus was built in Tudor Gothic style, a style commonly employed at American university campuses at the time. Rather than reference one university, however, Park may have referenced several when designing the new campus. The Main Hall and Central Library's Tudor arches, buttresses, and dormer windows are typical of the Tudor Gothic style.

Korea University Main Hall (left) and Central Library (right)

Space Group Building

Kim Swoo-geun is representative of the Korean architects of our time, together with Kim Chung-up. Kim Swoo-geun established his own theory about architectural space, rooted in Korean tradition—the third space, ultimate space, or womb space—that he skillfully put it into practice in the Space Group Building.

This building, his most exemplary work, is a complete break from his earlier architectural works, which tended toward formalism, such as the Freedom Center and the Walker Hill Hilltop Bar. The construction of the Space Group Building began in 1971 and was completed in 1977 after a new wing was added. The elegant flow of various spaces, a characteristic of traditional Korean architecture, took on a modern meaning in this work.

French Embassy

Kim Chung-up's French Embassy building is an example of adapting the later architecture of Le Corbusier to the local characteristics of Korea. In addition, Kim managed to strike a balance between the different characteristics of France and Korea.

The French Embassy building is ultimately Corbusian. Although both the architect and critics admit that the formal sensitivity was borrowed from Korea's traditional architecture, it is actually more correct to consider it an expansion or development of Corbusian architecture. The pure architectural space of early modernism that is so evident in Kim's Pusan National University and Sogang University Administration Hall, which were constructed around the same time, has developed into an ambiguous duality, and his creativity beyond Le Corbusier is most evident in the French Embassy building.

APPENDIX

INFORMATION

BOOKS

- Kim, Bongryol. *The Secret Spirit of Korean Architecture*. London, UK: Saffron Books, 2005.
- Yim, Seock-jae. *The Traditional Space*: *A Study of Korean Architecture*. Seoul: Ewha Womans University Press, 2005.
  [NB *The Traditional Space* is just one volume in Yim's *Study of Korean Architecture* series: other volumes include *Windows and Doors*; *Floral Lattices, Columns and Pavilions*; *Stone*, *Walls and Paths*; and *Roofs and Lines*.]
- Kim, Sung-woo. *Buddhist Architecture of Korea*. Elizabeth, NJ; Seoul: Hollym, 2007.
- Kim, Dong-uk. *Palaces of Korea*. Elizabeth, NJ: Hollym, 2006.
- Lee, Sang-hae. *Seowon: The Architecture of Korea's Private Academies*. Elizabeth, NJ: Hollym, 2005.
- The Korean Institute of Traditional Landscape Architecture. *Korean Traditional Landscape Architecture*. Elizabeth, NJ; Seoul: Hollym, 2007.
- Chun, Jin-Hee, et al. *Hanoak: Traditional Korean Homes*. Elizabeth, NJ: Hollym, 1999.
- Kim, Sung Hong, and Peter Cachola Schmal, eds. *Contemporary Korean Architecture*: *Megacity Network*. Berlin: Jovis, 2007.

MAGAZINES

Space: This monthly bilingual Korean and English magazine deals with architecture, urban design, interior design, and more. Published since 1966, it is well regarded in architecture circles worldwide. Its website (www.vmspace.com) is also full of good information.

ONLINE RESOURCES

- **KOREANARCHITECTURE.COM**
  www.koreanarchitecture.com
  An English-language "online community for open discussions on Korean architecture"
- **Asian Historical Architecture**
  www.orientalarchitecture.com
  Information on plenty of key South and North Korean buildings, all traditional with the exception of those in Pyongyang.
- **e-architect (Korea page)**
  www.e-architect.co.uk/korea
  Information on a large number of contemporary Korean buildings, mostly located in Seoul

PLACES TO VISIT

- **Bukchon Hanok Village**
  The collection of neighborhoods between Seoul's Gyeongbokgung and Changdeokgung palaces is renowned for its high concentration of *hanok* houses. Several of these have been converted into small museums introducing various aspects of Korean traditional culture. Bukchon Cultural Center (bukchon.seoul.go.kr), which offers a brief introduction to the basics of *hanok* and this area, is a good place to start. Come out of Exit 3 of Anguk Station, Seoul Metro Line 3, then take the first left.
- **Seochon**
  Though less systematically protected and touristy than Bukchon, the atmopsheric area between Gyeongbokgung Palace and Mt. Inwangsan also contains many *hanok*. Head north from Exit 1 or 2 of Gyeongbokgung Station, Seoul Metro Line 3.

- **Jeonju Hanok Village**
  A well-known collection of over 800 *hanok* in the southwestern city of Jeonju, popular among Jeonju locals and tourists alike for its traditional architecture, food, tea, and various cultural experience programs (tour.jeonju.go.kr).

TRADITIONAL ARCHITECTURE SCHOOLS

- **Cheongdo Hanok School**
  www.hanokschool.net | 82-54-373-8555
  This *hanok* school in Gyeongsangbuk-do has been open since 2003. It offers various courses, including full-time 12-week *daemok* (*hanok* structure building) and *somok* (*hanok* window frames, furniture etc) courses, a 12-week weekend self-build course, and more.

- **Korea Wood Builder College**
  builder.kr | 82-63-642-9922
  This school in Imsil, Jeollabuk-do, offers full-time three-month courses in traditional *hanok*, timber frame, and log construction, as well as *somok* and environmentally-friendly house construction.

- **Hwacheon Hanok School**
  www.hanokschool.co.kr | 82-33-442-3366
  Located in the mountains of Gangwon-do, this school also offers basic (six months) and intensive (three months; comes after completion of basic) courses in *hanok* building, as well as a 15-week weekend wood-framed earth house building course.

- **Korea House Traditional**
  www.hanok.co.kr | 82-33-333-3883
  Also in Gangwon-do, this school offers a full-time four-month course *hanok* building course.

- **Korea National University of Cultural Heritage (KNUCH)**
  nuch.ac.kr | 82-41-830-7114
  Unlike the other schools above, this institution offers full, four-year courses in traditional subjects like architecture, landscaping, and more.

These generally short courses (with the exception of those operated by KNUCH) should be regarded as basic introductions to a profession that is mastered mostly through professional experience: if you are serious about becoming a *hanok* builder, it is advisable to start working on *hanok* building sites soon after completing a course. All of the above courses are run in Korean, not English.

The content of this book is based on articles published in *Koreana* Vol. 12, No. 3, Autumn 1999. Introduction, Chapter 2, 3, and 4 were newly written by Ben Jackson, and Chapter 5 was written by Robert Koehler. Chapter 1 is an edited version of Kim Bong-ryol's article "Natural Perspective Revealed in Traditional Korean Architecture," while much of the information in Chapter 4 is based on Kim's seminal Korean series *Hanguk Geonchuk Iyagi* (*The Story of Korean Architecture*).

***Koreana* Vol. 12, No. 3, Autumn 1999**

"Natural Perspective Revealed in Traditional Korean Architecture" by Kim Bong-ryol
"The Path of Contemporary Korean Architecture" by Kim Kwang-hyun
"The Urban Environment and Architecture of Seoul" by Yim Chang-bok
"Korea's Modern Architecture of the 20th century" by Min Hyun-sik

PHOTOGRAPHS

Robert Koehler 7, 11, 24, 36, 37, 42, 43, 45, 47, 56, 58, 59, 60, 73, 74, 76, 77, 79, 80, 85, 92, 95, 96, 98, 99, 100, 101, 102, 103, 106, 107, 109, 111
Image Today 16, 17, 20, 21, 22, 23, 24, 28, 31, 33, 39, 41, 44, 48, 49, 52, 54, 56, 57, 63, 69, 70, 81, 105
Korea Tourism Organization 12, 14, 30, 31, 35, 38, 40, 58, 65, 71, 82, 84, 87, 90
Yonhap Photo 18, 27, 28, 35, 40, 50, 55, 67
Ryu Seung-hoo 8, 37, 75, 89

CREDITS

Publisher	Kim Hyunggeun
Writer	Ben Jackson, Robert Koehler
Editor	Lee Jin-hyuk
Copy Editor	Daisy Larios
Designer	Lee Bok-hyun